USS Tennessee (BB-43)

From Pearl Harbor to Okinawa in World War II

DAVID DOYLE

SCHIFFER MILITARY

4880 Lower Valley Road Atglen, PA 19310

Designed by Justin Watkinson
Type set in Impact/Minion Pro/Univers LT Std

ISBN: 978-0-7643-5668-1
Printed in China

Published by Schiffer Publishing, Ltd.
4880 Lower Valley Road
Atglen, PA 19310
Phone: (610) 593-1777; Fax: (610) 593-2002
E-mail: Info@schifferbooks.com
www.schifferbooks.com

For our complete selection of fine books on this and related subjects, please visit our website at www.schifferbooks.com. You may also write for a free catalog.

Schiffer Publishing's titles are available at special discounts for bulk purchases for sales promotions or premiums. Special editions, including personalized covers, corporate imprints, and excerpts, can be created in large quantities for special needs. For more information, contact the publisher.

We are always looking for people to write books on new and related subjects. If you have an idea for a book, please contact us at proposals@schifferbooks.com.

Acknowledgments

While working on this book I was blessed with the generous help of Tom Kailbourn, Tracy White, Sean Hert, Roger Torgeson, Rick Davis, James Noblin, Dana Bell, and Dave Baker. A special thanks is due to Paul Dawson, who along with his late wife, Karen, were instrumental in creating the USS *Tennessee* Museum in Huntsville, Tennessee, and were very generous in opening their vast resources for research. As always, I could have done none of this without the support of my wonderful wife, Denise, who took notes, scanned photographs, and accompanied me on numerous research expeditions. She truly is a great blessing to me.

Contents

Introduction

The battleship *Tennessee*, BB-43, that is the subject of this book was the sixth warship to bear the name of the sixteenth state. It was preceded by the 1854 sidewheeler; the unfinished Confederate ram that burned on the stocks in Memphis; the completed ram *Tennessee*, operated both by the Confederacy and the Union; the 1869 screw frigate *Tennessee*; and finally ACR-10, the 1906 armored cruiser that immediately preceded the *Tennessee* that is examined in this volume.

Completed too late for service in World War I, the *Tennessee*'s first combat was on the morning of December 7, 1941. Damaged but not sunk in the Japanese attack, the ship was repaired and saw action almost continuously throughout the war.

The most notable of BB-43's predecessors was the armored cruiser *Tennessee*, ACR-10. Launched at the William Cramp and Sons shipyard on December 3, 1904, the 14,500-ton warship was one of the most powerful warships in the world when commissioned on July 17, 1906. On May 25, 1916, the armored cruiser was renamed *Memphis* in order to make the name "Tennessee" available for the new battleship that is the subject of this book. *Memphis*, at anchor in shallow water in Santo Domingo harbor on August 29, 1916, was washed aground by a series of three massive waves, reaching up to 90 feet high, created by a hurricane. The ship was a complete loss, and forty-three of its men were killed, with a further 204 badly injured.

Armored Cruiser 10 was the fourth USS *Tennessee*, and when launched was one of the most powerful warships in the world. It was renamed USS *Memphis* on May 25, 1916, in order to free the name "Tennessee" for the new battleship 43. *Naval History and Heritage Command*

USS *Memphis* was lost when it was dashed upon the rocks in Santo Domingo harbor by a massive typhoon-driven wave. Forty-three men were killed or missing, and 204 were badly injured. There was heroism, too, with three of its crew being awarded the Medal of Honor. *Naval History and Heritage Command*

CHAPTER 1
Construction

The battleship *Tennessee* was constructed at the New York Naval Shipyard, also known as the Brooklyn Navy Yard. Here, the building ways have been prepared and decorated with patriotic bunting for the keel laying, the ceremony celebrating the official start of a ship's construction, on May 14, 1917. The United States had entered World War I about six weeks earlier. *National Archives*

Construction of the "new" USS *Tennessee*, along with a sister ship, was authorized by Congress on March 3, 1915. At that time the two ships were referred to merely as "Battleship 1916"—reflecting when construction was to begin. The congressional authorization stated: "The President is hereby authorized to have constructed two first-class battleships carrying as heavy armor and as powerful armament as any vessel of their class, to have the highest practicable speed and greatest desirable radius of action, and to cost, exclusive of armor and armament, not to exceed $7,800,000 each."

Bids for construction of the ships were solicited both from private industry as well as the Navy's own yards. When those bids were opened on November 17, 1915, there were responses from the private firms and three navy yards.

Two Navy yards presented the best values, and on December 8, 1915, Secretary of the Navy Josephus Daniels announced that battleship 43, the *Tennessee*, would be built at the Brooklyn Navy Yard, while its sister ship would be constructed at Mare Island Navy Yard. At that time, the battleship *California*, hull number 40, was also under construction in Brooklyn. However, bowing to public pressure, on March 14, 1916, the *California* in the building ways in Brooklyn was renamed *New Mexico*. The "Battleship 1916" to be constructed at Mare Island—battleship 44—would be *California*.

Battleship 43, the *Tennessee*, would be the lead ship of the class—the class thus being named the *Tennessee* class, and the Brooklyn yard would have overall responsibility for the design of both ships.

While originally planned for geared-turbine drive, less than a week after the contract was awarded, the decision was made to modify the contract and call for use of the turboelectric drive system that had previously been planned for installation in Battleship 1917.

Armament of the new warships would essentially duplicate that of the previous Battleship 1915; specifically twelve 14-inch rifles in four three-gun turrets, and a secondary battery of 5-inch guns that were mounted above the forecastle deck, augmented by deck-mounted antiaircraft guns.

The design of the ships was sufficiently satisfactory that the next year, four near duplicates, differing only in having eight 16-inch guns rather than twelve 14-inch guns, were ordered. One of the four ships of this follow-on group, known as the *Colorado* class, was not completed owing to the restrictions of the Washington Naval Treaty. While *Washington*, battleship 47, was not completed, *Colorado*, *Maryland*, and *West Virginia* were. These ships, collectively with *Tennessee* and *California*, came to be known as the "Big Five" and were the most powerful American battleships until the *North Carolina* class was commissioned in 1941.

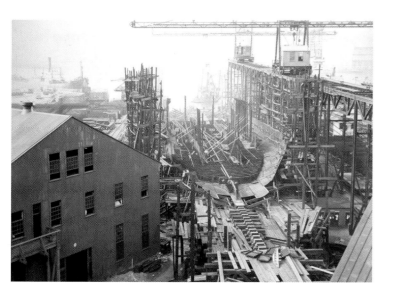

By July 5, 1917, construction of the lower part of the hull of the *Tennessee* was well underway. As viewed from above, shell (a.k.a. hull skin) plates and frame sections in the amidships area have been assembled at where the bow later would take shape. *National Archives*

Construction of the bottom of the stern has just begun in the foreground of this photo of work on the *Tennessee* dated October 5, 1917. At this stage of work, just a few wooden props support the stern; as work proceeded, more and more shoring would be needed to support the structure. *National Archives*

In another photo taken on July 5, 1917, the hull of the *Tennessee* is seen from the starboard quarter amidships, looking forward. Longitudinal bulkheads that will enclose the machinery spaces of the ship are being framed and cladded with steel plates. Many lateral frames on the hull bottom are in place; these were numbered from bow to stern, and number 104 is the closest one. *National Archives*

The bow in the foreground was beginning to take form when this photo was taken on October 5, 1917. To the right, a worker is guiding into place an I beam that a crane is lowering. Amidships, the bulkheads for the machinery spaces have risen to three levels high. *National Archives*

On a wintry February 4, 1918, a photographer ventured onto the aft crane of the building ways to photograph the progress on the *Tennessee* from above the stern, facing forward. In the foreground, bulkheads for many compartments are in place. Amidships, wooden planks and guard rails had been laid down temporarily on the transverse beams. *National Archives*

Two months later, in early April 1918, the progress of construction is shown from a similar perspective to that in the preceding photo. In the foreground are spaces that will house the steering gear and various storerooms and compartments. Surrounding the hull on three sides is scaffolding. *National Archives*

Several workers, including one wielding a sledgehammer, pose in the bow area of the *Tennessee* on August 1, 1918. Behind them is a transverse bulkhead marked "9," likely a reference to the frame it was located at. Farther aft, ladders are leaning on scaffolding erected to the front of another transverse bulkhead. *National Archives*

In a view of the construction of the *Tennessee* taken from Building No. 6 at the New York Naval Shipyard in May 1918, the entire hull is surrounded by wooden scaffolding, with only a bit of the upper part of the bow visible. On the trestle to the right are the two big cranes that delivered heavy components to the ship. *National Archives*

A photographer positioned in the bucket of the forward crane took this view of the *Tennessee* from over the bow, facing aft, on January 5, 1919. Canvas covers have been erected over the barbettes for turrets 1 and 2; the barbettes were the heavily armored tubes that would support the turrets and house their essential machinery and ammunition storage and hoisting facilities. *National Archives*

Also on January 5, 1919, a photographer took this image off the port stern, facing forward. The barbettes for turrets 3 and 4, still under construction, are covered with tarpaulins to keep out the elements. Other tarpaulins have been rigged here and there to offer some protection to workers and materials. *National Archives*

By April 1919, the upper deck, or forecastle deck, was framed, and deck plates were being installed on it. The view was taken from above the port beam amidships, facing forward. The barbette of turret 2 rises above the deck in the background; to the front of it is the opening for the barbette of turret 1. *National Archives*

Another of the photographs of *Tennessee* taken on January 5, 1919, faces forward from the port beam of the barbette of turret 3 (*far right*). Work on the hull was well advanced, as the top of the hull was nearing the top of the scaffold. *National Archives*

In early April 1919, workmen go about their business on the upper deck of the *Tennessee*. Steel deck plates have been secured in place, and various fixtures such as mooring bitts and hatches have been installed. A wooden frame over barbette 1 is available to throw tarps over in the event of foul weather. *National Archives*

One deck lower than the upper deck, and extending from the stem to the stern, was the main deck, shown here in a photograph taken off the port stern and dated April 1, 1919. Barbettes 3 and 4, with frames for tarpaulins over them, are in the foreground; rising in the background is the upper deck. *National Archives*

Workmen, some of whom were blurred during the long photographic exposure, perform their tasks on the fantail of the *Tennessee* on April 1, 1919, amid a tangle of air hoses, electrical cables, parts boxes, oxyacetylene bottles, and other necessary clutter. Lying on the deck are several unmounted mooring bitts and chocks. *National Archives*

The main deck is seen from the port aft corner of the upper deck on April 1, 1919. On the main deck, at the center of the photograph, is a motivational sign, reminding workers that the ship "goes over" or is to be launched on April 30, and that there were only twenty-nine days left before that date. *National Archives*

This view of the main deck facing aft on the *Tennessee* is part of a series of photos taken on April 29, 1919, one day before the ship was launched. At this point, the deck plates did not fit tightly against the unfinished barbette 3; these gaps would be closed later. On the starboard side of the deck, thick hawsers are laid out for use in the following day's launching. *National Archives*

In a photograph from the forecastle, facing aft on April 29, 1919, in the foreground are the entrances to the bullnoses: the tunnels through the bow through which the anchor chains hoisted and lowered the anchors. Shackled to the left is the starboard anchor, with its anchor chain lying slack along the deck. *National Archives*

Prior to the launching of the *Tennessee*, workers are engaged in constructing the first level of the superstructure above the upper deck. The photo was taken from the port side of the upper deck, facing aft, and in view are several of the casemates that will contain 5-inch/51-caliber guns of the secondary battery. *Naval History and Heritage Command*

With launching a day away, a worker on a ladder paints grid lines on the bow of *Tennessee*, apparently for reference or calibration during and after launching. Supporting the lower part of the bow was packing, also called poppets: temporary, form-fitting structures that would stabilize and support the bow as the ship slid down the ways and entered the water. *National Archives*

The forward packing on the port side of the hull is viewed from a closer perspective. Below the grid toward the right is the hatch for one of the 21-inch torpedo tubes that were located below the waterline. The torpedo tubes, one on each side of the hull, and their associated torpedo compartments later would be deemed a serious liability and eventually were eliminated. *National Archives*

The port side of the bow poppets attached to the *Tennessee* are viewed facing aft on April 29, 1919. The poppets were made of lumber and iron and were shaped to follow the contours of the hull. Heavy cables with turnbuckles, attached to moorings on the side of the hull, held the poppets in place. The poppets would be removed after the ship was launched. *National Archives*

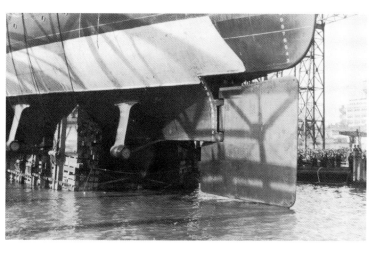

The stern packing for the *Tennessee* is seen from the port side. The light-colored paint on the hull indicated where the belt armor would be installed during the fitting-out. When its sister ship, the *California*, was launched, a lock was placed on the rudder to immobilize it, but no such lock is present on *Tennessee*'s rudder in this photo. *National Archives*

CHAPTER 2
Launching, Fitting Out, and Commissioning

On the morning of April 30, 1919, two weeks shy of two years after its keel was laid down, the *Tennessee* was launched. Shown here is the moment that the sponsor of the ship, Miss Helen Roberts, the daughter of the governor of Tennessee, christened the ship by breaking a bottle of champagne on the bow. *Library of Congress*

Twenty-three months after its keel was laid, on April 30, 1919, the massive form of *Tennessee*'s hull stood poised on the builder's ways of the Brooklyn Navy Yard, with Miss Helen Roberts, daughter of Tennessee governor Albert Roberts, ready to smash the traditional bottle of champagne, christening the ship and sending it down the ways into the water. Among the dignitaries in attendance was Assistant Navy Secretary Franklin Roosevelt, as well as Governor Roberts.

Shortly thereafter, the Navy approached the governor for help with a unique recruiting concept—to man the ship with recruits from Tennessee—known as the Volunteer State. The recruiting drive was considerably effective.

While the ship had been launched, and a recruitment drive had been initiated to man the warship, much work had to be done before it went to sea—or could even accommodate its crew.

Known as fitting out, the process of converting an empty hull into a complete seagoing vessel can take months, sometimes even years, finally culminating in a commissioning ceremony. In the case of *Tennessee*, the commissioning, when the vessel officially joins the ranks of US government warships, was on June 3, 1920.

Parading aboard that day were fifty officers, seventy Marines, and 1,026 sailors, including 631 from the state of Tennessee.

During shipyard trials in Long Island Sound, on October 30, 1920, one of the ship's two 300-kilowatt generators failed explosively, injuring two men and destroying the turbine end of the machine. Repairs illustrated that the designers failed to give consideration to the prospect of removing such a large piece of equipment from deep in the ship. Nevertheless, the ship's crew, shipyard personnel, and representatives of Westinghouse, who manufactured the gear, managed to complete repairs. In February 1921, it set out for more trials, after which it steamed for San Pedro, California, the port that it would call home for the next nineteen years.

Dignitaries on the christening stand along with spectators watch as the just-launched *Tennessee* glides through the water into Wallabout Bay. In addition to the thousands of spectators onshore, many people were assembled on the deck of the ship during the launching. Looming in the distance is the Williamsburg Bridge. *Library of Congress*

The *Tennessee* began its slide down the greased slipway at the New York Naval Shipyard at 0944. To arrive at this moment, it had been necessary for workmen to methodically knock out shoring holding the ship in place, until the weight of the ship initiated the slide. Note that the white grid was painted on the port side of the bow only. *Naval History and Heritage Command*

Dignitaries posing for their photograph after the *Tennessee* was launched included the ship's sponsor, Miss Helen Roberts, in the light-colored suit at the center; Assistant Secretary of the Navy Franklin Delano Roosevelt, in the top hat; and, to Roosevelt's side, Governor Albert H. Roberts of Tennessee. *Library of Congress*

Shortly after its launching, the hull of the *Tennessee* sits high in the water at the fitting-out dock at the New York Naval Shipyard. Here, construction of the ship would continue until its commissioning. The first level above the upper deck, called the 01 level, was under construction. The cage masts in the background belonged to another ship, probably *New Mexico*. *National Archives*

The *Tennessee* is seen from a slightly different perspective, moored to the fitting-out dock very soon after its launching. Water is being pumped out of two openings on the bow. *National Archives*

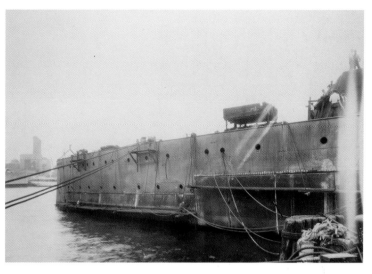

The aft part of the belt armor on the starboard side of the *Tennessee* is shown in an August 1, 1919, photograph. The rear edge of the belt armor had a smooth curve to the hull. Partially visible to the far right is the gunhouse of turret 4. *National Archives*

By the time this photo off the bow of the *Tennessee* was taken on August 1, 1919, the belt armor had been installed. Running along both sides of the hull above and below the waterline, the belt armor ranged in thickness from 13.5 inches down to 8 inches. It was designed to defeat shells and torpedoes that struck the vulnerable waterline area. *National Archives*

In another photograph from August 1, 1919, some of the belt armor on the forward starboard part of the *Tennessee* is in view, extending to slightly above the staging planks. The top of the dark-painted area of the hull on the right side of the photo marks the completed ship's waterline. *National Archives*

This photograph of August 1, 1919, tells us much about the status of construction on the *Tennessee* three months after its launching. For example, the gunhouses and the 14-inch/50-caliber guns of turrets 1, 3, and 4 had been installed. The heavily armored conning tower and part of the superstructure were taking shape above the 01 level. *National Archives*

The superstructure of the *Tennessee* is viewed from the port side of the 01 level, or superstructure deck, on August 1, 1919. Two men are standing next to the massive block of a crane as a heavy component is being lowered into the space below. *National Archives*

The uptake from the boilers to the smokestack (*lower right*) is seen from the superstructure deck on August 1, 1919. The uptake was of faceted design and heavily armored. The view is facing across the ship from the port side of the deck. *National Archives*

Another of the August 1, 1919, photographs of the *Tennessee* shows turret 1 from the forward part of the upper deck, facing aft. In the foreground is steel deck plating that later will be covered with wooden decking. In the background is US Navy Floating Derrick No. 21. *National Archives*

In a final photograph from the August 1, 1919, series, turret 3 is seen from the rear of the upper deck, facing aft. The reason for the white dots with consecutive numbers painted below them on the barbette is unclear, but these markings were present on all four barbettes at this time. *National Archives*

Facing forward from the fantail of the main deck on August 1, 1919, turret 4 is traversed to port. Above turret 4 is turret 3, its guns pointing to starboard. Beyond is the superstructure. *National Archives*

A photograph dated September 1, 1919, focuses on the bow of the *Tennessee* at the fitting-out dock at the New York Naval Shipyard, showing the three bullnoses for the anchors and, above them, the two hawser holes for the hawsers that moored the ship to a dock. *National Archives*

A September 13, 1919, photograph shows the king post of the port boat crane installed amidships, surrounded by scaffolding, but the boom of the crane is not yet installed. At the top of the superstructure is the box-shaped pilothouse, which soon would be surrounded by an enclosed bridge. *National Archives*

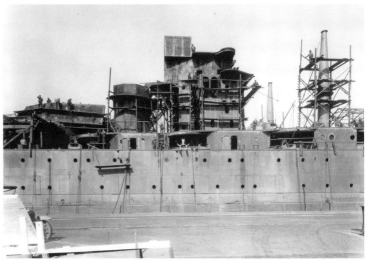

The port side of the superstructure is the focus of this September 13, 1919, photograph. From left to right are turret 2, the conning tower, the superstructure, and the king post of the port boat crane. Later, the smokestack will be constructed between the superstructure and the boat cranes. *National Archives*

The faceplates at the fronts of turrets 1 and 2 had not yet been installed when this photo of the *Tennessee* was taken on October 1, 1919. The boom of the port boat crane now has been installed and is drooping downward to the rear of the crane king post. *National Archives*

The *Tennessee* is viewed off the port bow at the fitting-out dock in an undated photo apparently taken between early October 1919 and the end of that year. The boom has been installed on the king post of the port boat crane, and an enclosed navigating bridge with large, rectangular windows has been installed around the pilothouse at the top of the superstructure. *Naval History and Heritage Command*

A dock crane lowers a load of lumber onto the upper deck of the *Tennessee* in an undated photo probably taken sometime between early October 1919 and the end of that year. The boot topping, a black band along the waterline that was intended to disguise floating oil, which tends to collect on the hulls of ships in harbors, has been applied. *Naval History and Heritage Command*

Extensive wooden staging, or scaffolding, is erected around the superstructure of the *Tennessee*, seen from the starboard side, in a photo dating to late 1919. Exterior platforms for the various levels of the superstructure are yet to be built. Toward the right, workers go about their business atop the heavily armored conning tower, the navigational and fire-control center of the ship during battle. *Naval History and Heritage Command*

Work was still underway on the superstructure and other exterior structures and systems when this view of the *Tennessee* was taken on January 2, 1920. Tarpaulins were draped over the still-open gunhouses of turrets 1 and 2. Visible between the superstructure and the boat crane is the aft smokestack. *National Archives*

As seen in another photograph dated January 2, 1920, the top of the conning tower, not present in a September 1919 photo from a similar perspective, now was finished and is visible here in a line of sight from the lower part of the jack staff on the bow. *National Archives*

The *Tennessee* appears to be nearing completion in this photo. The faceplates on turrets 1 and 2 are now present. The cage masts also appear to be nearly completed, with scaffolding still present around them. The boilers are fired up and producing steam. *Naval History and Heritage Command*

Now flying a jack from the jack staff, the *Tennessee* has now been commissioned, earning it the right to bear "USS" (United States Ship) before its name. The commissioning ceremony, during which the ship was formally transferred to the US Navy, was held on June 3, 1920, a little over three years after construction of the ship commenced.
Library of Congress

Officers of USS *Tennessee* pose on deck around the time of the ship's commissioning. The ship's first commander was Capt. (later Admiral) Richard H. "Reddy" Leigh, who served in that post until 1921. He is the officer kneeling at the center of the group, with four stripes and a star on each sleeve. *Library of Congress*

Some of the crewmen of USS *Tennessee* are lined up on the quarterdeck with their bedding and effects. The original crew at the time of the commissioning were nicknamed "plank owners." Many of the enlisted crewmen were recruited in the state of Tennessee. *Naval History and Heritage Command*

On the newly commissioned battleship *Tennessee*, officers and civilians mingle on the main deck in the foreground while, in the background, throngs of shipyard workers perform their tasks on the platforms and fighting top of the mainmast. *Library of Congress*

The USS *Tennessee* is in port shortly after its commissioning. A few sailors dressed in whites are on scaffolding along the side of the hull, apparently scraping the sides or applying paint: a never-ending task on any ship. Bedding or tarpaulins are draped over the rails to dry out.
Naval History and Heritage Command

The USS *Tennessee* was photographed from the Manhattan Bridge in New York City as it took its first trip under its own power in open waters, on October 15, 1920. The purpose of the trip was to salute the Atlantic Fleet off Staten Island.

A New York Naval Shipyard photograph dated February 2, 1921, shows a Vickers-type broadside-firing director attached for training purposes to the mount of a 5-inch/51-caliber gun of USS *Tennessee*'s secondary battery. *National Archives*

USS *Tennessee* departs from New York City on February 26, 1921, en route to Guantánamo Bay, Cuba, for standardization trials. The ship carried a quantity of boats of different sizes on the superstructure deck, including a sizeable barge abeam the superstructure. *National Archives*

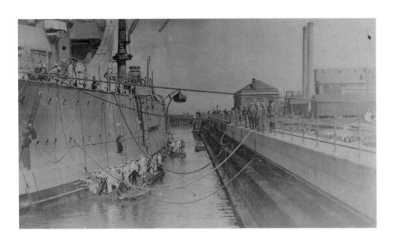

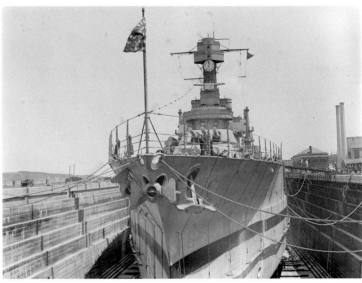

Following its operational trials at Guantánamo, the *Tennessee* steamed north to Boston, Massachusetts, where it underwent work in drydock in April 1921. Once the ship had entered drydock and was moored, the first step was for sailors to board planks suspended from the ship and scrape marine growth and corrosion from the hull below the waterline as the water was pumped out of the drydock, as seen here. *Boston Public Library*

Mooring lines are still attached to the ship and the drydock. The ship was carefully positioned over an array of massive blocks and timbers on the floor of the drydock to support the immense weight of the ship. Staging planks are suspended from lines along the hull for men to stand on while preparing the hull for repainting. *Boston Public Library*

At the navy yard in Boston, the *Tennessee* is resting in the drydock. By now, the hull below the waterline had been scraped and the water had been completely pumped out of the drydock. Now, the way was clear for performing any major repairs to external components below the waterline. *Boston Public Library*

USS *Tennessee* is viewed from astern during its drydocking at the navy yard in Boston in April 1921. The ship's name was painted in dark letters, probably black, on both sides of the stern. The ship was being put into condition for its full-power trials off the coast of Maine the following month. *Boston Public Library*

The hull below the waterline of the *Tennessee* had been painted a light color since its launching, but in drydock in Boston in 1921 it was entirely repainted in a dark color, presumably red, as seen in this view from astern dated April 29, 1921. In the right foreground are the keel blocks that supported the keels of ships in drydock. *National Archives*

Sailors and shipyard workers pose near the starboard propellers of USS *Tennessee* while other sailors on the planks above apply paint to the hull, in drydock at Boston on April 29, 1921. Major repairs were done on one of the ship's generators and the number 4 motor during this drydocking. *National Archives*

Men on staging planks paint the hull below the waterline on the USS *Tennessee* while the ship is in drydock at Boston in April 1921. This work was done the old-fashioned way, with paintbrushes. A clear view is available of the three anchors housed in the bullnoses. *USS Tennessee Museum*

During its sea trials in May 1921, USS *Tennessee* is anchored off the Rockland Breakwater Lighthouse on the Maine coast. During these trials, the ship made a series of high-speed runs to test its endurance and ability to achieve high speeds without mechanical breakdowns. *National Archives*

Thick, black smoke billows from the smokestacks of USS *Tennessee* during a high-speed run off Rockland, Maine, during the May 1921 sea trials. The view is from the port side of the upper deck, facing aft, with a casemate to the lower left and a 5-inch/51-caliber gun above it. The stacked boats are marked "TENN" on the bows. *USS Tennessee Museum*

A photo of the *Tennessee* in drydock at the San Francisco Naval Shipyard at Hunter's Point in the summer of 1921 illustrates an interesting design feature of its hull. On the lower part of the hull, abeam turret 2, is a large, fin-shaped object: one of four on the hull, with two more on the aft part of the hull abeam turret 3. These apparently served a similar purpose to bilge keels: long, continuous fins that act to prevent the ship from rolling. *National Park Service*

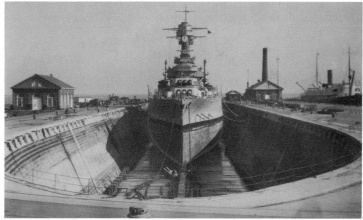

In May 1921, the USS *Tennessee* proceeded to its new home port of San Pedro, California, via the Panama Canal, and the following month, a year after it was commissioned, the ship underwent a series of sea trials to test its ability to achieve a specified speed of 21 knots. The *Tennessee* was able to exceed that speed. It is shown during a speed run on June 21. *University of Memphis*

USS *Tennessee* rests in drydock at the San Francisco Naval Shipyard, in a view off the bow. Flexible spouts, probably made of canvas, were attached at three points on each side of the hull, above the waterline, to divert expelled water away from the hull while it was undergoing painting. Atop the navigating bridge is a rangefinder, above which on the foremast below the fighting top is the forward range clock, a device for silently signaling the firing range of a target to trailing ships. *National Park Service*

USS *Tennessee* is anchored off Vancouver, British Columbia, in August 1921. By now, azimuth scales had been painted on turrets 2 and 3. Comprising a scale with numbers on a black background, these scales were intended to let fire-control personnel on nearby friendly ships know the azimuth the primary-battery guns were set at, in order to more quickly lay their own guns. *City of Vancouver Archives*

Tennessee is seen from a slightly different angle during its visit to Vancouver in August 1921. A huge canvas awning had been erected over the main deck from the mainmast to the stern. Atop turret 3 is the aft main-battery rangefinder, complementing the forward main-battery rangefinder atop the navigating bridge. *City of Vancouver Archives*

USS *Tennessee* is viewed from a rowboat off Vancouver, British Columbia, in August 1921. The ship arrived in that port on the fifth of the month. In making its way to Vancouver, the battleship had visited Tacoma and Seattle, Washington, in July. *City of Vancouver Archives*

In October 1922, the USS *Tennessee* is docked at the Navy Yard, Puget Sound (NYPS), at Bremerton, Washington. Capital ships of the United States Battle Fleet, based at San Pedro, California, often were dispatched to NYPS annually for repairs and modernization. *Puget Sound Naval Shipyard*

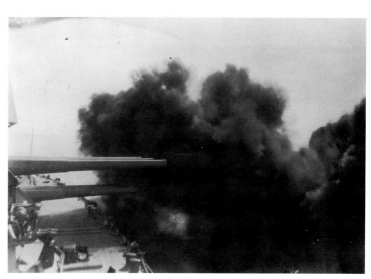

USS *Tennessee* unleashes a low-elevation broadside salvo with its 14-inch/50-caliber guns. When elevated to an angle of 15 degrees, these guns were capable of sending a 1,400-pound armor-piercing shell approximately 13.6 miles. It took 470 pounds of propellant to fire the shell. *USS Tennessee Museum*

In a photo of the *Tennessee* taken in the early 1920s, canvas awnings are rigged over many of the spaces on its main deck and upper or forecastle deck. A boat boom is extended on the side of the hull, and a boat is moored to it. Boat booms were the means of securing the various boats that always were deployed when a battleship was in port. *National Archives*

Members of the crew of USS *Tennessee* have decorated their quarters with a fake fireplace and garlands of evergreen branches to celebrate Christmas 1923 at the Navy Yard, Puget Sound. Sailors were often ingenious in their efforts to make their surroundings as cheerful as possible. *USS Tennessee Museum*

Boxing was a very big deal in the US Navy throughout most of the twentieth century, with frequent boxing matches held on ships and at bases, with championships at stake. Here, a pair of pugilists duke it out in a ring on the deck of the *Tennessee* as officers, sailors, and a few civilian spectators enjoy the match. *USS Tennessee Museum*

Canvas awnings are rigged on the *Tennessee* to protect personnel on deck from the intense rays of the sun. This photo dates to around 1924, since there is a catapult on the fantail, and this apparatus was installed on the ship sometime in 1924. *USS Tennessee Museum*

With boat booms swung out and awnings rigged, *Tennessee* lies at anchor in February 1924. Old Glory flies from the flagstaff, as prescribed for a ship at anchor. *USS Tennessee Museum*

A boat on davits and an extended boat boom cast shadows on the hull of USS *Tennessee* while underway at low speed sometime in March 1924. For 1923–24, the crew of the ship scored an "E" for excellence in gunnery and won the Battle Efficiency Pennant for attaining the highest scores in gunnery and engineering. *National Archives*

During a transit of the Panama Canal by the *Tennessee* in 1924, sailors lounge on the upper deck, the bridges, and the roofs of the turrets. The 14-inch gun barrels have been polished to a high sheen, and tompions are inserted in the gun muzzles. In the foreground is a clear view of the wildcats: the upper parts of the anchor windlasses. *USS Tennessee Museum*

In the early 1920s, the Navy equipped many of its battleships and cruisers with catapults for launching scout planes. The catapult installed on the fantail of the *Tennessee* in 1924 has one of the ship's two assigned Vought UO-1 scout planes on it. To the right is the derrick-type aircraft crane for hoisting the scout planes aboard and onto the catapult. *USS Tennessee Museum*

USS *Tennessee*'s Vought UO-1 number 1 is about to be launched from the catapult in 1924. Naval doctrine called for employing battleship-launched scout planes as spotter aircraft, to transmit information to enable the ship's batteries to place indirect fire on distant targets. *USS Tennessee Museum*

Vought UO-1 number 1 from USS *Tennessee* and a Vought VE-7H from the cruiser USS *Milwaukee* (CL-5) fly in close formation. *Tennessee*'s UO-1 number 1 was the first aircraft to be assigned to the ship; it was assigned USN Bureau Number A6607. *National Museum of Naval Aviation*

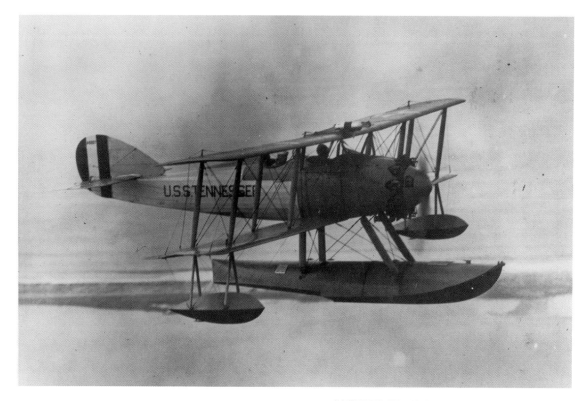

Also assigned to USS *Tennessee* was this Vought UO-1, Bureau Number A6867. The Bureau Number is faintly visible on the rudder at the top of the white stripe. Initially, battleships carried a second scout plane on the ship to provide cover for the spotter plane. *National Museum of Naval Aviation*

Whenever a USN ship crossed the equator, members of the crew—from officers down to enlisted men—who had not previously "crossed the line" endured initiation rites known as a Neptune Party or Line-Crossing Party. These crewmen, known as Pollywogs, were hazed before being promoted to Trusty Shellbacks. A Neptune Party is in full swing on the *Tennessee* in this photo captioned "Shellbacks All" from the 1920s. *USS Tennessee Museum*

A 1924 view from the main top of USS *Tennessee* includes, in the distance, its sister ship, USS *California* (BB-44). In the foreground is a good view of the foretop, which included spotting and fire-control compartments for the primary and secondary batteries atop the foremast. *USS Tennessee Museum*

The aft port corner of the upper deck is the scene of a part of the revelries in a USS *Tennessee* Neptune Party in which an initiate is being shaved as members of Neptune's court look on. These revelries, although quite farcical, were and remain an important part of the Navy's traditions. *USS Tennessee Museum*

Although the rituals of a Neptune Party might vary depending on circumstances, one typical one was to dunk the Pollywogs into a tank of saltwater, such as the one shown here aboard USS *Tennessee*. This one was fashioned from timbers, netting, and canvas. *USS Tennessee Museum*

A sailor poses next to one of the *Tennessee*'s casemates during a cruise off the coast of Mexico in 1924. Visible within the casemate port are the mount and part of the barrel of a 5-inch/51-caliber gun, and, to the right, several sailors. *USS Tennessee Museum*

The saltwater tank used in a Neptune Party on *Tennessee* is viewed from the quarterdeck, facing forward to the port aft corner of the main deck. One of the ship's early crossings of the equator occurred during its 1925 cruise to Australia. *USS Tennessee Museum*

The crew of one of the *Tennessee*'s 3-inch/50-caliber antiaircraft guns conducts a drill. To the right, carriers bring up fixed ammunition (meaning the shell and the powder cartridge were one assembly). *USS Tennessee Museum*

Sister ships USS *Tennessee*, foreground, and USS *California*, in the background, are anchored next to each other sometime in 1925. *California* wears the gunnery "E" for excellence awarded to the ship for 1925–26 on the aft smokestack. Three scout planes are aboard the *Tennessee*. *National Archives*

In a photo taken from an aircraft from Naval Air Station Pearl Harbor, Territory of Hawaii, on April 27, 1925, USS *Tennessee* and other ships engage in a mock bombardment of shore defenses in advance of an amphibious landing. Less than two decades later, the ship would engage in such operations in earnest. *National Archives*

This aerial photograph of USS *Tennessee* was taken from an airplane of the 11th Photo Section, based in Hawaii Territory, on June 5, 1925. Curiously, four scout planes are aboard: two in tandem on the catapult and one on each side of the catapult. A canvas awning was rigged over the forecastle deck, forward of turret 1. *National Archives*

USS *Tennessee* is moored to USS *Medusa* (AR-1), the first purpose-built repair ship to enter USN service. *Medusa* earned the nickname "Floating Navy Yard." *Medusa* was commissioned in September 1924, and according to a label on the photograph it was taken in 1927. Note the sailors priming the hull above the boot topping. *USS Tennessee Museum*

USS *Tennessee* rides at anchor in an aerial photo dated March 1930. A light-colored circle, probably a temporary identification symbol, is painted on the foredeck between the anchor chains. Three scout planes are on the ship: one on the fantail, one on the fantail catapult, and one on a second catapult installed on top of turret 3 in 1928. Note the positioning of the rangefinder on top of turret 2, offset to the left side. *National Archives*

Santa Claus comes to the USS *Tennessee*. At Christmastime 1932, a tree has been positioned on the quarterdeck, and Santa, to the left of center in the foreground, is distributing presents to orphan children who are guests of the crew. Even during the depths of the Great Depression, the crew of *Tennessee* did their part to ease the suffering of the unfortunate. *USS Tennessee Museum*

Members of Fire-Control Division of USS *Tennessee* pose for a group portrait on the fantail of the ship in 1933. Several trophies are displayed on the deck. To the side are two of the ship's Vought O3U-1 scout planes stowed in tandem on the catapult. *USS Tennessee Museum*

On a sunny Sunday morning, a church service is being held on the quarterdeck of the *Tennessee*. Religious life was an important part of the spiritual well-being of many members of the crew. In the foreground atop turret 3 are two of the ship's O3U-1 scout planes, including Bureau Number 8573 with markings for Observation Squadron 3 (VO-3). *USS Tennessee Museum*

One of the *Tennessee*'s motor whaleboats is being hoisted aboard the ship by a boat crane in fairly rough seas. The abbreviated name of the ship, "TENN," is painted on each side of the bow of the whaleboat. *USS Tennessee Museum*

In a 1930s view aft from the port side of the forecastle deck, in the foreground is a deck winch for hauling on hawsers, to the rear of which a 5-inch/51-caliber gun barrel protrudes from a casement cover. Above that casement is another 5-inch/51-caliber gun on the superstructure deck. *USS Tennessee Museum*

In an oblique aerial view of USS *Tennessee* taken on May 31, 1934, the mainmast from the top of the aft fire-control station (below the searchlight platform) to the bottom of the maintop was painted black. This was called a black smoke band, and painting these bands on cage mainmasts to hide soot from the smokestack had been the practice in the battle fleet for some time. *National Archives*

A scout plane on the turret 3 catapult is seen close-up from the mainmast of the *Tennessee*. The plane apparently was a Vought O3U. A small number "5" is painted on the engine fairing, below the propeller. The opaque, rather than the usual clear, windscreen for the observer's cockpit is noteworthy. *USS Tennessee Museum*

This snapshot of sailors at horseplay to the front of one of the *Tennessee*'s 5-inch/51-caliber guns was inscribed by the original owner, "Jakich and I sky-larking. McGrath referee. Taken by gun 8 on April 21, 1934, at Conon, C.Z. [Canal Zone]." *USS Tennessee Museum*

The black paint on the upper half of the mainmast of USS *Tennessee* is particularly prominent in this photograph of the ship at anchor at San Pedro, California, in April 1935. The top rims of the smokestacks also were painted black. *National Archives*

Another snapshot from the same source, taken on the forecastle of the *Tennessee*, is inscribed, "Sight-seeing from top of No. 1 and No. 2 turrets, going through Panama Canal on April 24, 1934." In the foreground is a hatch leading to the crew's berthing on the main deck, one level below. A transit through the canal was always an event of interest to the crew and something that broke up their sometimes-monotonous routines. *USS Tennessee Museum*

On June 11, 1937, the *Tennessee* became grounded on mud flats off Alameda, California, while maneuvering toward an anchorage. Navy tugs maneuver to pull the battleship loose, with Angel Island and the San Francisco–Oakland Bay Bridge in the distance. A close examination of the photo indicates that the aft fire-control station on the lower half of the mainmast is now absent. Also gone now was the rangefinder atop turret 2. The extended platform and bulwark are now present around the middle level of the maintop. *National Park Service*

Various divisions of the ship's company dressed in blues are assembled on the deck of the *Tennessee* around the mid-1930s. The ship's number, 43, is painted in a light color, probably white, on the roof of turret 2 but is difficult to discern. The aft fire-control station on the mainmast below the searchlight platform is still present but would be removed soon. Also, the middle level of the maintop would, by 1937, receive a new platform with a bulwark around it. *National Park Service*

The tugboat *Sea King* is being positioned alongside the *Tennessee*'s aft port quarter while another tugboat is situated forward of the *Sea King*. The absence of the aft fire-control station on the mainmast is very noticeable from this angle. *National Park Service*

A tugboat maneuvers along the port beam of *Tennessee* during its grounding off Alameda. On the starboard side, several of the ship's boats are moored to the boat boom. The port anchor is lowered. By the time this photo was taken, tubs for .50-caliber antiaircraft machine guns had been emplaced on the front and the rear of the middle level of the foretop. *National Park Service*

In a view of two of *Tennessee*'s Curtiss SOC-3s from the left side, their USN Bureau Numbers are visible on the vertical fins: 1077 for 2-O-1 and 1076 for 2-O-2 are seen from the side. "TENNESSEE" is marked on the fuselage, just forward of and below "U.S. NAVY." The flying-pelican insignia of VO-2 is on the forward part of the fuselages. *Naval History and Heritage Command*

By July 1938 the *Tennessee* had been assigned three Curtiss SOC-3 scout planes, all three of which are present in this photo. They were numbered 2-O-1, 2-O-2, and 2-O-3. The planes were from Observation Squadron 2 (VO-2), which was attached to Battleship Division 2 (BatDiv2). Each has an E for Excellence on the side of the cockpit. Both cockpits were fully enclosed, and protective covers are secured over the canopies. *Naval History and Heritage Command*

USS *Tennessee* is docked at the Puget Sound Navy Yard during periodic repairs, maintenance, and modernization on January 20, 1939. The black object to the front of the superstructure apparently is a temporary exhaust stack for a heater or other combustion equipment. *Puget Sound Naval Shipyard*

Apparently little had changed in the exterior appearance of USS *Tennessee* from the time it was photographed at Bremerton, Washington, in January 1939, and when this photograph of the ship was taken at Bremerton on July 15, 1940. Mk. 19 directors had been mounted on the platform above the navigating bridge; these served to control the secondary battery as well as the searchlights. A rangefinder remained at the front of that platform. *Puget Sound Naval Shipyard*

On the morning of December 7, 1941, Imperial Japanese naval air forces executed a surprise attack on Oahu, Territory of Hawaii, with the main goal of destroying the US battleships at Pearl Harbor. In this photo taken by a Japanese photographer in the first moments of the attacks, geysers from two torpedoes are visible among the battleships along the far shore of Ford Island. Among the ships moored there was USS *Tennessee. National Archives*

Aggression by Germany and Japan had made it clear that the United States would soon be drawn into war. Hoping at least to prepare for this, or at best to avert war, the United States Fleet conducted Fleet Problem XXI in 1940. The war games were to be close enough to Japan to be noticed, but not so close as to be perceived as a threat. The fleet's base of operations for this maneuver would be Hawaii. On April 1, 1940, the battle fleet sailed from its time-honored home of San Pedro–Long Beach, bound for Hawaiian waters.

The exercise concluded, the fleet was scheduled to sail for San Diego on May 16, 1940, but two days prior to sailing the fleet was instead ordered to Lahaina Roads, the fleet's deepwater anchorage off Maui.

Following the successful use of aerial torpedoes by the British against the Italian fleet in Taranto in the Adriatic, it was decided that the Lahaina Roads anchorage was too vulnerable to that type of attack. The fleet instead would begin to anchor in Pearl Harbor, whose shallow depth it was believed made it invulnerable to aerial-launched torpedo attacks.

With that thought in mind, the fleet settled into a routine of one week of maneuvers followed by two weeks tied up in harbor, with *Tennessee*'s usual spot being interrupted quay Fox Six (F-6), adjacent to Ford Island.

Tennessee was tied up inboard of fellow Big Five battleship *West Virginia* (BB-48) at F-6 on the morning of December 7, 1941, when the Japanese struck. Directly behind the *Tennessee* was the ill-fated *Arizona* (BB-39).

Aboard *Tennessee*, General Quarters was sounded, watertight doors closed, guns manned, boilers lit, and preparations made to get underway. *West Virginia*, stricken by Japanese torpedoes, began to sink. Concerned that it would capsize, as had *Oklahoma* (BB-37), moored outside *Maryland* (BB-46), moored ahead of *Tennessee* at Fox Five, counterflooding was ordered on the *West Virginia*. This allowed it to settle evenly to the shallow bottom of the harbor, sparing it the fate of *Oklahoma*, but pinning *Tennessee* firmly against the concrete mooring quays.

Flames from burning oil atop the harbor, fed by the ruptured tanks of *Arizona* and *West Virginia*, lapped the stern of *Tennessee*. Trapped against the quay, *Tennessee*'s engines were ordered ahead, the propellers not moving the ship, but rather pushing the flaming oil away from its hull. At about 0758, *Tennessee* was hit by the first of two bombs. One of these hit the top of turret 3, after first tearing through the catapult. The bomb partially penetrated the turret and, while not exploding, did start a fire, killing and injuring men. At 0810 a second bomb struck, this time hitting the center gun of turret 2. Shell splinters killed one man on the *Tennessee* and two aboard *West Virginia*, including its captain, Mervyn Bennion.

Aboard *Tennessee*, the Japanese attack had killed three men immediately (a fourth dying later from injuries) and injured twenty-five, and two men were missing. Despite the loss of these men, *Tennessee* and its crew fared better than many that day.

On December 16, the mooring quays were dynamited, freeing the ship, which eased forward through the berth previously

In the aftermath of the Japanese attack on Pearl Harbor on December 7, 1941, the USS *Arizona* (BB-39) burns in the foreground, with USS *West Virginia* (BB-48) and, inboard of it, USS *Tennessee* in the background. *Tennessee* was protected from torpedo strikes by the *West Virginia* and suffered two nonfatal bomb hits. *National Archives*

USS *West Virginia* and, behind it, USS *Tennessee* are viewed from a different angle on December 7, 1941. By the time this photo was taken, burning fuel oil from USS *Arizona* was edging closer along the surface of the water toward both ships, but crewmen fended off the flames by spraying them with water. *National Archives*

occupied by *Maryland*, passing abreast the sunken *West Virginia* and *Oklahoma*.

After some hasty repairs, *Tennessee* along with *Maryland* and *Pennsylvania* left Pearl Harbor bound for the mainland. *Tennessee* arrived at Puget Sound Navy Yard on December 29.

The next month the damaged main battery guns were replaced, the main mast was removed, and all portholes were plated over. Additional antiaircraft defense in the form of 20 mm guns were added. With the pressing need to have the ship ready for service, little more was done at this time. However, in February 1943, the ship returned to Puget Sound for an extensive modernization. *Tennessee*'s superstructure was removed to the second deck. Replacing the cage mast and twin funnels would be a single funnel and a modern conning tower, resembling that of the *South Dakota*-class battleships. The conning tower was actually taken over from a cruiser design, due to weight considerations. Adding to the *South Dakota* resemblance was the installation of eight 5-inch/38-caliber twin mounts and radar-equipped secondary-battery directors. These dual-purpose weapons would not only be effective against surface targets but would also give considerable weight to *Tennessee*'s antiaircraft defenses. Providing additional protection from further aerial aggression was a battery of 40 mm guns in fourteen quad mounts, and additional 20 mm automatic cannons. Significantly, antitorpedo blisters were added to the hull, increasing its beam to 113 feet, 11⅞ inches, precluding its passing through the Panama Canal. The rebuild was extensive, and it would be May 8 before the reconfigured battlewagon could undergo sea trials. At the conclusion of those trials, it departed for Adak, Alaska.

In the aftermath of the December 7, 1941, attack on Pearl Harbor, the *West Virginia*, foreground, has settled in the water, while, to the inboard side of it, the *Tennessee* remains fully afloat. The two ships' two-color Measure 1 camouflage schemes are clearly visible. *National Archives*

USS *Tennessee* was photographed from off the starboard bow at its mooring at Berth F-6 on December 7, 1941, as smoke billowed from the destroyed USS *Arizona* in the background. Splinters from a bomb hit on the center gun of turret 2 damaged not only the gun and the faceplate of the turret, but also parts of the front of the superstructure and its bulwarks and the air-defense platform. *National Archives*

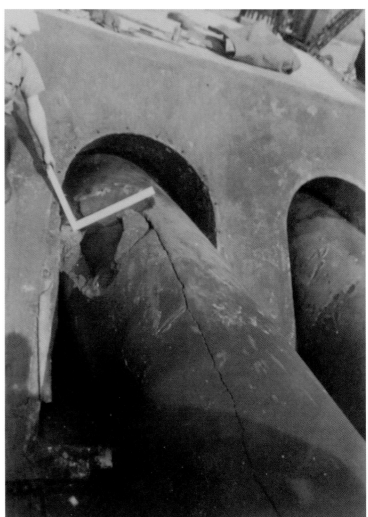

A sailor holds a framing square against the large gouge where a Japanese bomb detonated against the center 14-inch gun barrel of turret 2. The explosion destroyed the gun as well as caused damage to nearby structures. *National Archives*

In a December 10, 1941 photo, the sunk *West Virginia* has the *Tennessee* jammed against the upper part of the forward quay of Berth F-6 at Pearl Harbor. To free the ship from its berth, it would be necessary to carefully dismantle the forward quay through a series of blasts. *National Archives*

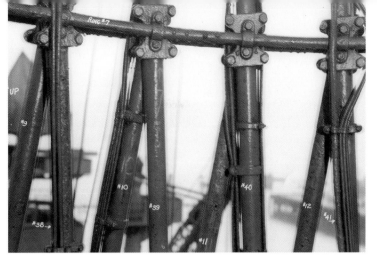

Once the *Tennessee* was freed from Berth F-6 and temporary repairs were made to it, the ship proceeded under its own power to the Puget Sound Navy Yard for major repairs and modernization. It arrived there on December 29, three weeks after the attack on Pearl Harbor, and was docked at Berth 6-C. This photo, taken at PSNY on January 10, 1942, provides details of the cage-type mainmast, scheduled for removal, showing one of the rings and some of the clamps that secured the main elements—the crisscrossing pipes—where they intersected. *National Archives*

Another view of the destruction rendered to the center gun of turret 2 (*right*) shows how the bomb blast blew away the bloomers of all three guns of that turret and wrecked the frames that secured the bloomers to the front plate of the turret. *National Archives*

As this January 17, 1942, PSNY photograph of the cross sections of five main-element pipes from the *Tennessee*'s mainmast demonstrates, the pipes had suffered from varying degrees of corrosion, with the walls of the pipes quite thin in some areas. *National Archives*

By February 19, 1942, when this overhead photo of the *Tennessee* was taken, the cage mainmast had been replaced by a tower; a small mainmast with yardarms was now mounted on the rear of the aft smokestack. The original cage foremast and fighting top would remain. All of the main-battery guns had been replaced by new 14-inch/50-caliber guns: Mk. 11. *National Archives*

The *Tennessee* is viewed toward the stern from off the port beam on February 19, 1942. On the former site of the cage-type mainmast there was now a tower containing a vegetable locker, searchlight and machine gun platforms, and the aft fire-control stations. Shields made of STS (special-treatment steel) were installed on the 5-inch antiaircraft gun mounts, and the guns were thoroughly overhauled. *National Archives*

As seen in a February 19, 1942, photo showing the bow of the *Tennessee* from above, during the repairs at PSNY, the center wildcat, anchor chain, and anchor had been removed and the deck where the wildcat had been was now plated over. A safety grille was installed over the center hawse pipe. The two parallel lines visible hanging aft of the anchor are for the paravanes, one of which is visible on the port deck edge aft of the large bits. *National Archives*

The *Tennessee* is anchored in Puget Sound on February 26, 1942, the day after it departed from the navy yard, bound for San Francisco. The catapult and roof on turret 3 had been damaged by a bomb blast on December 7, 1941, but both items had been replaced. The new structure, containing a vegetable locker and platforms for searchlights and machine guns, is just forward of turret 3. Nonessential boat skids had been removed. *A. D. Baker III collection*

An aerial view of the port side of USS *Tennessee*, taken shortly after it left PSNY in early 1942, shows three Vought OS2U Kingfisher scout planes aboard. At PSNY, the ship had been fitted with SC and FC radar equipment as well as FD equipment less the antennas. *National Archives*

By February 1942, all but a few of the portholes on the hull had been covered with welded plates. Shell plating on the hull that had buckled during the Pearl Harbor attack had been repaired. The .50-caliber and 3-inch antiaircraft guns had been replaced by a new battery of 20 mm and 1.1-inch automatic antiaircraft guns. Atop the forward fighting top, the new SC "bedspring" air-search antenna is clearly visible.
A. D. Baker III collection

During *Tennessee*'s post–Pearl Harbor repairs at PSNY, part of the main deck was "re-wooded": that is, given new planking. At PSNY, the ship had been given a new camouflage paint scheme: Measure 11; modified to use 5-N Navy blue instead of the original 5-S Sea Blue on all vertical surfaces and the somewhat darker Deck Blue (20-B) on horizontal surfaces. *National Archives*

The *Tennessee* casts a long shadow in this aerial photo taken off the stern around late February 1942. The new aft fire-control stations on the short tower just forward of turret 3 were much lower than the original stations atop the cage mainmast. To the port side of the barbette of turret 3, a 20 mm gun mount within a splinter shield is visible; forward of that mount on a raised platform with a splinter shield is a quad 1.1-inch antiaircraft gun mount. *National Archives*

The *Tennessee* is viewed from above the bow in another photo dating to around late February 1942. The SC air-search radar antenna is in view above the forward fighting top, and faintly visible below that antenna, on the roof of the fighting top, is the FC fire-control radar antenna. *National Archives*

The *Tennessee* cruises in open waters in the first half of 1942. Here, the FC radar antenna is clearly visible atop the forward fighting top, with the less visible SC radar antenna towering above it. Stacked life rafts are stowed on the sides of the turrets and on the superstructure deck. *National Archives*

USS *Tennessee* is viewed from directly overhead in a photograph taken in or around June 1942. The red circles on the national insignia on the Kingfisher scout planes on the ship's fantail recently had been deleted. A close examination of the photograph discloses a quad 1.1-inch antiaircraft gun mount on a round platform with a splinter shield on each side of the forward part of the superstructure. *National Archives*

Another aerial photo of the *Tennessee* around June 1942 was taken from above the stern. The tub for a single 20 mm antiaircraft gun on the main deck to each side of turret 3 and the larger tubs for a quad 1.1-inch gun mount to each side of the aft fire-control tower are clearly visible. *National Archives*

Tennessee is viewed from astern in a circa June 1942 photo. The ship's number, 43, is painted in white on each side of the stern. Bloomers were not fitted on the 14-inch guns where they emerged from the frontal plate of the turret at this point in time. Tubs had been added to the upper parts of the king posts of the boat cranes, each with a .50-caliber antiaircraft machine gun. *National Archives*

This aerial view of the *Tennessee* was taken within a moment of the immediately preceding photo, as indicated by the placement of personnel on the main deck. Some of the new gun shields for the 5-inch antiaircraft guns on the superstructure deck are in view; they protected the crews from splinters from the front, above, and the sides but not the rear. *National Archives*

Another aerial view of *Tennessee* was taken during the same flyover as the preceding several photos, since the exact same groupings of men and officers are on the decks. Two Vought Kingfishers are on the fantail and the catapult, but the catapult above turret 3 is empty. *National Archives*

A final aerial view from around mid-1942 captures the *Tennessee* from off its starboard bow. Now possessing a more modern suite of weaponry and radar equipment six months after the Pearl Harbor attack, the battleship was finally ready to enter the fray. *National Archives*

USS *Tennessee* returned to Pearl Harbor from August 14 to 18, 1942, to take on provisions, fuel, gasoline, and fresh water. The ship is viewed from above on the eighteenth, moored to Berth F-8 on Battleship Row and surrounded on all sides by torpedo nets. Forward of the *Tennessee* are the sunken ruins of USS *Arizona* alongside Berth F-7. *National Archives*

The *Tennessee* slices through the waves sometime during 1942. During this period, the *Tennessee* did not see combat, being engaged largely in training exercises off the West Coast. The battleship also made voyages to Hawaii in June and August. Its next stop would be the Puget Sound Navy Yard for a major rebuilding. *Puget Sound Naval Shipyard*

At the end of August 1942, rebuilding work on the *Tennessee*, which would last until early May 1943, commenced at the Puget Sound Navy Yard. The model of the *Tennessee* in this photograph dated March 20, 1943, represents the changes made to the battleship: most noticeably, the new superstructure with a single smokestack adjoining the rear, new aft primary- and secondary-battery directors, and the addition of eight twin 5-inch/38-caliber gun mounts. *National Archives*

As seen in the model of the rebuilt *Tennessee*, the conning tower immediately aft of turret 2 was shortened, the tower of the superstructure that contained the bridge and the primary-battery director was now positioned more aft, and the forward secondary-battery director was positioned between the top of the conning tower and the front of the superstructure tower. *National Archives*

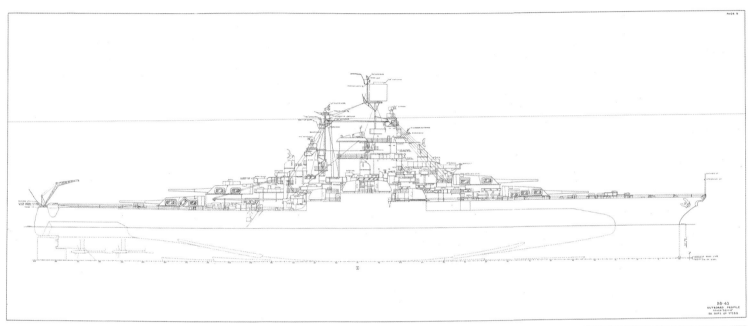

BB-43
OUTBOARD PROFILE
SCALE 1/8"=1'-0"
50 SHIPS UP STERN

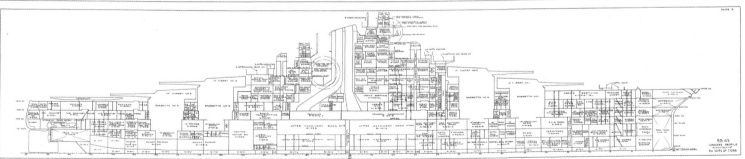

BB-43
INBOARD PROFILE
SCALE 1/8"=1'-0"
50 SHIPS UP STERN

The new superstructure of USS *Tennessee* is seen from the port side on May 1, 1943. At the top of the superstructure is the new, forward Mk. 34 primary-battery director. On the low tower aft of the smokestack is the aft Mk. 34 director. Three of the four new Mk. 37 secondary-battery directors are visible: at the front of the superstructure, abeam the smokestack, and to the rear of the aft Mk. 34 director. An SG-2 surface-search radar antenna was on the foremast, aft of the forward Mk. 34 director, and the SC-2 air-search radar antenna is on the new mainmast, attached to the front of the aft director tower. *National Archives*

The starboard Mk. 37 director is viewed facing aft at PSNY on April 30, 1943. The director had a lightly armored enclosure for its crew and was fitted with hatches, viewing ports, and, protruding from the sides, an optical rangefinder. On top of the director was an antenna for a Mk. 4 radar, used for acquiring and tracking targets. *National Archives*

This PSNY photo, taken on April 30, 1943, from the port side, shows a side view of the forward Mk. 34 main-battery director, with the antenna for a Mk. 8 fire-control radar on top of the housing. To the rear of the director atop the foremast are the SG surface-search radar antenna and, above it, the "ski pole" antenna for the IFF (identification, friend or foe) set. *National Archives*

Newly rebuilt USS *Tennessee* lies at anchor off the Puget Sound Navy Yard on May 8, 1943. The ship now presented a noticeably more modern appearance; from this angle, the new, tapering superstructure tower is seen to good advantage. Gone were the casemates for 5-inch/51-caliber guns on the first level of the superstructure. *Puget Sound Naval Shipyard*

Ten quad 40 mm antiaircraft gun mounts were installed on the *Tennessee* during the 1942–43 refitting. Two of these were on platforms faired into the stern of the ship abaft the aircraft crane. A new aircraft crane was installed on the fantail, and the catapult atop turret 3 had been removed; two 20 mm antiaircraft guns in tubs were now atop turret 3. *National Archives*

As seen from off the stern in another May 8, 1943, photo at PSNY, antitorpedo blisters were now present on the sides of the hull. These blisters, which improved the ship's stability as a gun platform and added protection against torpedo and shell hits, had the effect of increasing its beam from 97.5 feet, as built, to 114 feet. The ship was now too wide to ever again transit the Panama Canal. *National Archives*

In a May 8, 1943, view off the bow of the *Tennessee*, it is possible to see the contours where the new hull blisters were faired into the original part of the hull, forward of turret 1. Another consequence of the widening of the hull was that it accommodated the new twin 5-inch/38-caliber gun mounts. *National Archives*

USS *Tennessee* cruises at speed just after its 1942–43 rebuilding. The top of the forward part of the port hull blister is visible from below the forward twin 5-inch gun mount to below the muzzles of the 14-inch guns of turret 1. Above the top of the blister to the immediate front of the forward 5-inch mount is a curve in the hull, designed in large part to accommodate the 5-inch mounts. *National Archives*

This photo of USS *Tennessee* in Puget Sound on May 12, 1943, was marked up to indicate the locations of the various radar and IFF antennas on the ship. BK IFF antennas are on the port yardarm of the foremast and the starboard yardarm of the aft fire-control tower. FD, or Mk. 4, antennas are on the Mk. 37 directors. FH, or Mk. 8, radar antennas are atop each of the two Mk. 34 main-battery directors. The SG surface-search radar antenna is atop the foremast. The SC-2 air-search radar antenna is barely visible atop the mainmast, just aft of the smokestack. A BL-2 IFF antenna is on the rail along the rear of the smokestack. *National Archives*

USS *Tennessee* conducts a speed run off Port Angeles, Washington, on May 12, 1943. This was part of sea trials to ascertain the ship's performance capabilities following its major renovations. A new feature was the group of three 20 mm antiaircraft guns in tubs on the forecastle. *A. D. Baker III collection*

As viewed from astern, the *Tennessee* conducts a speed run off Port Angeles on May 12, 1943. The ship had yet to take aboard its complement of scout planes. On the main deck to each side of turret 3 was a recently installed quad 40 mm gun tub and a 20 mm gun tub. *A. D. Baker III collection*

The *Tennessee* was photographed from above its bow as it attained a speed of 20 knots on May 12, 1943. During the speed trials, the ship achieved a maximum speed of 20.6 knots. The 20 mm guns on the forecastle were arranged in two adjoining tubs: a single gun was in the front one, and the other two were in the wider tub to the rear. *A. D. Baker III collection*

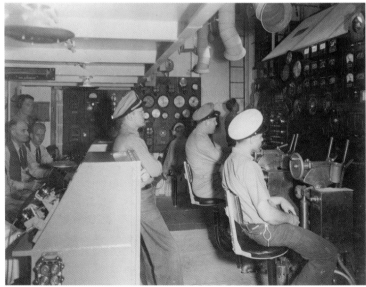

The propulsion control room of USS *Tennessee* was photographed during the trials on May 12, 1943. This room contained the equipment for effecting the centralized control and coordination of the ship's complex electrical-propulsion systems. To the left are several civilian engineers who were consulting during the ship's trials. *National Archives*

Following its sea trials, USS *Tennessee* received orders to proceed to Alaskan waters to patrol along with Task Force 16.22.1 against possible Japanese movements in the Bering Sea and the Aleutian Islands. Here, the ship is at anchor in Iliuliuk Bay, Unalaska, on July 20, 1943. *National Archives*

In August 1943, USS *Tennessee* is anchored in the foreground off Adak in the Aleutian Islands. The cruiser USS *Louisville* (CA-28) is the larger of the ships in the background. *National Archives*

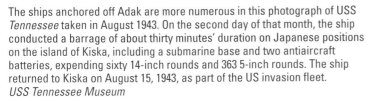

The ships anchored off Adak are more numerous in this photograph of USS *Tennessee* taken in August 1943. On the second day of that month, the ship conducted a barrage of about thirty minutes' duration on Japanese positions on the island of Kiska, including a submarine base and two antiaircraft batteries, expending sixty 14-inch rounds and 363 5-inch rounds. The ship returned to Kiska on August 15, 1943, as part of the US invasion fleet. *USS Tennessee Museum*

One of the several OS2N-1s assigned to USS *Tennessee*, number 21, is hauled onboard, with the pilot and the observer onboard. The hoist cable from the aircraft crane was secured to a fitting above the pilot's headrest. The observer's compartment was armed with twin .30-caliber machine guns, visible under the aft section of canopy. *USS Tennessee Museum*

One of USS *Tennessee*'s OS2N-1s (similar to the Vought OS2U-3 but built by the Naval Aircraft Factory) approaches the ship for recovery. There were several types of possible scout-plane recovery procedures: this one appears to be a "Dog" recovery, in which the ship made a sharp turn in order to create a calm patch of sea for the plane to land and taxi on. *USS Tennessee Museum*

Several months after the Alaska expedition, USS *Tennessee* crossed the equator on October 26, 1943. The traditional Neptune Party, or Line-Crossing Party, was interrupted when two tragedies struck. A seaman, K. V. Munson, was fatally wounded when he was crushed in an accident in turret 2. A half hour later, the ship's OS2N-1 number 21 accidentally slid off the catapult and crashed into the sea, killing the pilot, Lt. Harry Chapman. Here, personnel on a small craft alongside the upended plane are attempting to render assistance. *USS Tennessee Museum*

USS *Tennessee* participated in the bombardment of Tarawa, which began just hours before the USMC landings on that atoll on November 20, 1943. Despite the tons of shells fired on the small, tightly defended island of Betio in the atoll, the Japanese were able to marshal a fierce resistance to the landings. A post-battle analysis determined that the ships had bombarded the island at too great a range and had begun the barrage too soon before the landings. Changes in USN bombardment doctrine resulted from this fiasco. Some of the shore installations and shell and bomb craters on Tarawa are shown in this aerial view. *USS Tennessee Museum*

A photograph of USS *Tennessee* steaming off Pearl Harbor on December 13, 1943, upon its return from Tarawa shows it still painted in the by-now-war-weary Measure 21 camouflage scheme it had received earlier that year. The ship would soon receive a new camouflage measure. *National Archives*

Shortly before this aerial photo of the *Tennessee* was taken on December 29, 1943, the ship returned to San Pedro, California, where work began repainting the ship from Measure 21 camouflage to Measure 32/1D. As can be seen by a comparison of this photo with the following two, only part of the repainting work had been completed by December 29. *National Archives*

By the time this photo of *Tennessee* was taken on January 11, 1944, at San Pedro, California, the repainting of the ship in Measure 32/1D was complete, or nearly so. Crewmen involved in the painting recalled that Measure 32/1D was a particularly laborious camouflage to apply.
National Archives

Another view at San Pedro, probably taken on January 11, 1944, provides another view of the Measure 32/1D camouflage on *Tennessee*'s port side. This measure comprised patterns of Light Gray (5-L), Dull Black (BK), and Deck Blue (20-B) overall, but with Ocean Gray (5-O) and Deck Blue (20-B) on horizontal surfaces.
National Archives

USS *Tennessee* is viewed off its port stern at San Pedro on or around January 11, 1944. Measure 32 camouflage was intended to mask the identity and course of the ship and thus confound enemy submarine attacks.
National Archives

As viewed from astern at San Pedro, the lighter colors of the stern, the aft turrets, aft directors, and parts of the smokestack and forward superstructure stand in contrast with the darker colors of the hull patterns and the 5-inch/38-caliber gun mounts.
National Archives

An aerial view of the port side of USS *Tennessee* depicts the horizontal surfaces as painted in the ship's new Measure 32/1D scheme. Although somewhat difficult to discern, the prevalent color on the decks and horizontal surfaces was Deck Blue, with the lighter Ocean Gray appearing in swaths on the port side of the forecastle and the fantail, and at several other locations. *National Archives*

USS *Tennessee* is seen from farther aft in an aerial photo taken around early January 1944. Measure 32 camouflage and its variants saw widespread use in the Pacific Theater in 1944. *National Archives*

In a final view of the *Tennessee* taken at San Pedro, California, on or around January 11, 1944, the Measure 32/1D patterns as viewed from the front are clearly visible. A small number "43" is painted in white on the bow. The hull blisters added about a year earlier are plainly discernible. *National Archives*

In the center background, USS *Tennessee* participates in the bombardment of Parry Island in Eniwetok Atoll, Marshall Islands, in support of US landings on February 20, 1944. Drawing on lessons learned from the Tarawa invasion, the *Tennessee* carried out its shelling much closer to shore: so close that it even employed its 40 mm antiaircraft guns against Japanese positions. *National Archives*

One of the Kingfishers of USS *Tennessee* has been hoisted back onboard, and crewmen are struggling to position the plane on the catapult sled. The pilot is exiting the cockpit. To the right is the tail of another Kingfisher. *USS Tennessee Museum*

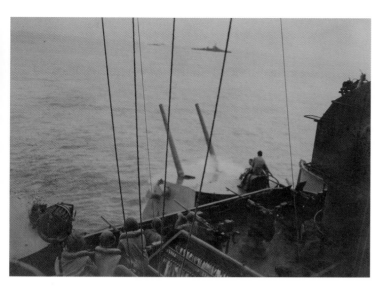

While *Tennessee* was bombarding Japanese positions on Saipan at around 0914 on June 15, 1944, three Japanese 6-inch shells simultaneously struck the ship. One hit a gun port of the aft starboard (or number 7) twin 5-inch/38-caliber DP gun mount. Smoke is issuing from that port, as viewed from the flag bridge, with the starboard flag locker in the foreground and a 20 mm antiaircraft gun gallery just below. To the far right is the starboard, or number 3, Mk. 37 director. *USS Tennessee Museum*

The front of the number 7 twin 5-inch/38-caliber DP gun mount is seen after a 6-inch shell struck it. The shell entered the right gun port, detonating on the right gun tube just inside the frontal shield, and the blast disabled the gun crew inside, killing eight men. *USS Tennessee Museum*

Another Japanese 6-inch shell struck the main deck of *Tennessee* at frame 98, 13 feet to starboard from the centerline. A hole 36 inches by 26 inches was blown through the deck, and there was other damage from shrapnel. Some of the damage is viewed from the rear of the 01 level, facing aft. *USS Tennessee Museum*

One of the three six-inch shells to hit *Tennessee* penetrated the hull blister at frame 89 on the starboard side, blowing a hole 40 inches high by 34 inches wide about 18 inches above the existing waterline. This photo shows a patch welded over the hole, with the approximate shape of the shell hole chalked on it. *USS Tennessee Museum*

The top and frontal plates of the gunhouse of 5-inch/38-caliber gun mount number 7 have been unbolted and removed, exposing the damaged interior. Among items in the gun mount that were destroyed by the Japanese shell were five telephone headsets, one jack box, two lighting fixtures, and cable leads to the right rammer motor. *USS Tennessee Museum*

Smoke rises from the shore during USS *Tennessee*'s shelling of Garapan town and Tanapag Harbor, Saipan. The *Tennessee* was involved in the bombardment of Saipan from D-1, June 14, to D+7, June 22, 1944. Sometime between the first of the year and then, a new, taller foremast had been installed to the front of the smokestack, topped with a big, new SK air-search radar antenna and, above it, an SG surface-search radar antenna. *National Archives*

After Saipan and repairs at Eniwetok, USS *Tennessee* proceeded to Guam, where it joined with Task Unit 53.5.3 in the bombardment of the island on July 20, one day before the invasion began. Here, USS *Tennessee* lies off the coast of Guam during an apparent lull in the action. During *Tennessee*'s first full day off Guam, for example, the ship provided covering fire for underwater demolition teams, firing 168 14-inch rounds, 428 5-inch rounds, and 2,730 40 mm rounds. *USS Tennessee Museum*

On July 23, 1944, USS *Tennessee* shifted from Guam to Tinian, where for the next week it fired on shore targets. Here, the ship is pounding Japanese positions on Tinian with a salvo from its aft 14-inch guns, as photographed from astern from USS *California*. *National Archives*

After the bombardment of Tinian, the *Tennessee* returned to Guam for another week of fire-support operations. This photo of the ship was taken from USS *New Mexico* (BB-40) during the Guam operations in July 1944. *National Archives*

At 0434 on August 23, 1944, while cruising with Task Unit 53.5.4 in the open sea, the *Tennessee* suffered a failure in one of the steering motors, rendering the ship out of control. Sixteen minutes later, while the crew was trying to regain steering control, the *Tennessee*'s stem collided with the bow of USS *California*. The damaged *Tennessee* arrived at Espiritu Santo the following day, where it is seen at anchor at Berth 16 in Segond Channel. *USS Tennessee Museum*

As seen from the forecastle of the *Tennessee,* the collision with the *California* caused a series of dents to the top of the starboard side of the hull above the wooden deck and damage to the chock to the right. To the left is the starboard anchor chain. That anchor had added to the damage to the *California* as it bashed against its hull during the collision. *USS Tennessee Museum*

Collision with *California*

Tennessee joined *California* and *Pennsylvania* on August 12, 1944, as did eight cruisers and destroyers, to form Task Unit 53.5.4, and they steamed for the New Hebrides, pausing on August 21 for a "Crossing the Line" ceremony presided over by "King Neptune."

The revelry gave way to tragedy just before dawn on Wednesday, August 23. While steaming at 16 knots, the bridge of *Tennessee* lost steering control at 0434 hours. Three minutes later, control was regained with the auxiliary steering gear, with the ship having already swung widely off course. Using the air motors of the auxiliary steering gear, the ship had begun to be brought back on course, when steering control was lost again at 0446. Bearing down on its sister ship *California*, at 0448 the Commander Battleship Division Two radioed "Steering casualty on Imperial"— indicating *Tennessee* had lost steering control. At 0449, *Tennessee*'s engines were ordered to back down emergency full, and the side lights were turned on. *Tennessee*'s deck log shows that at 0451, Collision Quarters was sounded, one minute after its bow plowed into the side of *California* at about frame 21.

The sound of rending steel shattered the night as the two ships met and swung to parallel courses, coming into contact over about two-thirds of their lengths, before finally the reaction to the impact pushed them apart.

Understandably, both ships were damaged in the collision, with *California* faring the worse, with eight men either killed or going over the side, never to be seen again.

Aboard *Tennessee*, the starboard hull plating was ripped open just behind the anchor, and the number 1 5-inch mount was badly damaged, one barrel being bent.

Tennessee returned to Espiritu Santo, arriving on August 27, for repairs by the crew from the repair ship USS *Aristaeus*, ARB-1.

An investigation into the cause of the collision revealed that the initial problem was caused when a pin in the *Tennessee*'s steering motor sheared off. Control was transferred to the significantly slower but effective auxiliary steering gear while repairs were made to the main steering gear. During the course of that repair, the main gear was reconnected 180 degrees out of alignment. When control was shifted back to the main gear, it was immediately overloaded and failed. While no men aboard *Tennessee* were killed in the collision, as mentioned that was not the case on *California*.

Tennessee's Capt. Mayer, who just a few weeks earlier was awarded a Bronze Star in part for his seamanship at Saipan, lost his command. At the same time, the navigator, Cmdr. Bruce Ware, was removed as well. Temporary repairs to *Tennessee* were completed on September 2, and the ship proceeded toward the Solomon Islands.

The stem and the bow of the *Tennessee* are viewed from a closer position after its collision with USS *California*. Most of the damage was to the starboard side of the bow and the hull. *USS Tennessee Museum*

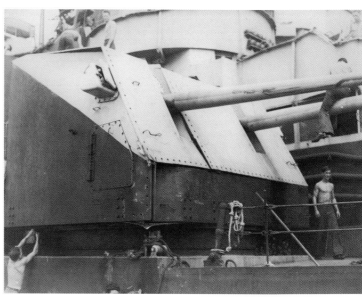

The number 1 twin 5-inch/38-caliber gun mount (the forward one on the starboard side) was damaged in the collision with the *California*. Screws holding the side and frontal plates together were sheared, the upper forward part of the side plate was pushed in, and the right gun was twisted inboard. *USS Tennessee Museum*

The collision with the *California* resulted in a large rent in the starboard side of the *Tennessee*'s hull, which was repaired at Espiritu Santo. Although the *Tennessee* suffered no personnel losses from the collision, the *California* suffered seven killed and one missing. *USS Tennessee Museum*

The *Vulcan*-class repair ship USS *Hector* (AR-7) is moored along the starboard side of USS *Tennessee* at Espiritu Santo, effecting repairs caused by the collision with USS *California*. Following the repairs, which consumed about a week, *Tennessee* departed Espiritu Santo for the bombardment of Angaur, in Palau. *USS Tennessee Museum*

This photo is thought to show USS *Tennessee* conducting a bombardment of the island of Angaur (now Ngeaur Island) in the Palau Group in September 1944. The ship has just executed a tight turn to port, and the guns of turret 2, traversed to starboard, have just fired a salvo. *USS Tennessee Museum*

American aircraft bomb Japanese positions on a beach on Angaur. The *Tennessee* participated in the shelling of this island for eight days in September 1944 in support of the hard-fought US invasion of Peleliu. *USS Tennessee Museum*

Surigao Strait

On October 25, 1944, *Tennessee* took part in what would ultimately be the last battleship-versus-battleship combat. A few days prior, on October 17, Allied forces began to land on islands in the Leyte Gulf, in the central Philippines. This action was part of a plan to interrupt the supply of fuel needed by the Japanese war machine. The Japanese responded by developing a strategy to lure the American fleet away from the invasion beaches by using the Imperial Japanese Navy (IJN) carrier fleet as bait. If successful, this would leave the Allied landing force exposed, and open to attack by IJN surface forces under Vice Admirals Shoji Nishimura, Kiyohide Shima, and Takeo Kurita.

The Japanese "Southern Force" including the battleships *Yamashiro* and *Fuso*, the heavy cruiser *Mogami*, and four destroyers, all under Nishimura, were to strike through Surigao Strait.

However, the Americans were aware of the Japanese plan, and at 1443 on October 24, 1944, VAdm. Thomas C. Kinkaid sent a brief message to RAdm. Jesse Oldendorf, reading, "Prepare for night engagement." Oldendorf, flying his flag from the cruiser *Louisville*, commanded 7th Fleet Support Force, Task Groups 77.2 and 77.3. At his disposal was a formidable armada, including six battleships. Five of these, including *Tennessee*, were Pearl Harbor veterans. Joining *Tennessee* were battleships *West Virginia*, *Maryland*, *Mississippi*, *California*, and *Pennsylvania*, plus four each of heavy and light cruisers, twenty-eight destroyers, and thirty-nine PT boats.

The US battleships had spent the past several days conducting shore bombardments, and the crews were well honed. Additionally, *Tennessee*, *California*, and *West Virginia* had modern and effective Mk. 8 range keepers and Mk. 8 fire-control radar. Oldendorf positioned his heavy ships to block Surigao Strait, the passage between Leyte Island and Dinagat Island, and positioned first his PT boats followed by his destroyers up the strait, forcing the Japanese to run a gauntlet. RAdm. G. L. Weyler commanded the battle line from *Mississippi*. At about 0300, both Japanese battleships were struck by torpedoes fired by US destroyers, with DD-680 *Melvin* sinking *Fuso*. At 0302, *Tennessee*'s search radar made contact with one large ship at a range of 43,900 yards. At 0313, with the range closed to 37.500 yards, *Tennessee*'s main battery plot had a firing solution and was ready to fire. Three minutes later, *West Virginia*'s main battery opened fire on the Japanese, the first American battleship to do so.

Because the ships had originally been dispatched to shell shore installations, none of the battleships had many armor-piercing shells aboard. In order to conserve this ammunition, the decision was made to hold fire until the enemy was closer. Finally,

Activity on the quarterdeck of USS *Tennessee* is documented in this photo taken while the ship was anchored at Seeadler Harbor, Manus Island, on September 28, 1944. Judging from the expectant look of the crew members and the ramp and carpet on the deck to the right, a VIP was about to board the ship. To the left, a sailor sits on the left side of the rangefinder of turret 3. To the lower right is a demarcation between the darker Deck Blue paint and the lighter Ocean Gray. *USS Tennessee Museum*

at 0355 and a range of 20,500 yards, *Tennessee*'s 14-inch rifles opened up on the leading Japanese ship, the *Yamashiro*.

At 0402 *Tennessee*, steaming at 15 knots, ceased fire and swung around, its main battery turrets pivoting to they could again be brought to bear on the enemy. At 0407 it resumed fire; one minute later it received the order to cease fire, by which time it had fired sixty-nine 14-inch rounds at the enemy.

The Japanese force was decimated; Nishimura's flagship *Yamashiro* sank about 0420, with him aboard. At dawn only two of Nishimura's ships remained, with *Mogami* being abandoned at 1047 and scuttled two hours later, leaving only *Shigure* as a survivor of the Japanese Southern force.

Oldendorf's ships withdrew, preparing to face the Japanese Southern Force—the Second Striking Force, under VAdm. Shima. However, Shima, approaching the strait, encountered the withdrawing and sinking *Mogami* and what he believed to be the wrecks of both Japanese battleships, and wisely chose to retreat. Thus, the night fight of October 25 became the last gunfight between battleships.

While providing fire support against Japanese positions on Leyte in the Philippines on the evening of October 21, 1944, USS *Tennessee* was accidentally rammed by the transport ship USS *Warhawk* (AP-168). The bow of the *Warhawk* is seen here where it struck the port side of *Tennessee*, between frames 114 and 118. *USS Tennessee Museum*

The damage to the *Tennessee* is viewed from another angle. Later on October 22, the USS *Potawatomie* (AT-73), a fleet tug, would come alongside the ship, and its crew would perform repairs to the *Tennessee*'s blister, and the battleship would be back in full service the morning of the twenty-third. *USS Tennessee Museum*

The damage from the collision with *Warhawk* is documented in this photo. The crash crumpled the plating of the hull blister on the aft side of the hole, accordion style. The blister did its job, protecting the interior of the ship from flooding. *USS Tennessee Museum*

After seeing combat at the Battle of Surigao Strait, the last time battleships would fight against battleships, the *Tennessee* returned to the Puget Sound Navy Yard for repairs and modernization in late 1944. During that sojourn, one of the ship's Vought Kingfishers, number 22, flies above Washington State. *USS Tennessee Museum*

Tennessee is off the Puget Sound Navy Yard on January 25, 1945. During its time in the yard, the ship had been repainted in Measure 21, the same scheme the ship had worn in 1942 and 1943. On this date, the ship underwent recalibration of its radar systems. *National Archives*

The *Tennessee*'s superstructure is viewed from the starboard side in a photograph taken at the Puget Sound Navy Yard on January 21, 1945. A change worthy of notice is the SP height-finding and low-angle search radar antenna on top of the mainmast. *National Archives*

The aft directors and the smokestack are observed from the aft starboard quarter. The Mk. 4 radar antennas had been replaced on the Mk. 37 secondary-battery directors with the Mk. 12 antenna, with the Mk. 22 parabolic or "orange-peel" antenna jutting from its right side. The number 4 Mk. 37 director is to the far left. *National Archives*

A closer look at the new SP height-finding and low-angle search radar antenna on top of the mainmast of the *Tennessee* is provided in this January 21, 1945, photograph at the PSNY. On the end of each of the yardarms extending from the top of the mast are IFF (identification, friend or foe) antennas: a BK on the left and BM to the right. A worker is operating on the platform under the SP antenna. *National Archives*

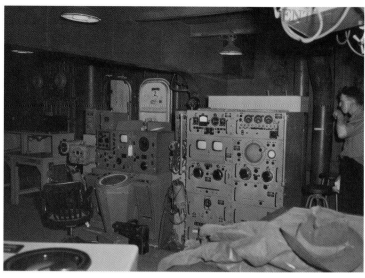

The combat information center of a warship had radar, plotting, and communications equipment and a specially trained staff tasked with plotting and tracking enemy threats above, on, and below the sea. The *Tennessee's* CIC is shown facing aft in a photo from January 21, 1945.
National Archives via James Noblin

This somewhat visually cluttered view is from alongside the aft or number 4 Mk. 37 director (*right*) facing the aft Mk. 34 primary-battery director. Mounted on top of the director is the FM radar antenna. Above the director is PSNY's hammerhead crane. *National Archives*

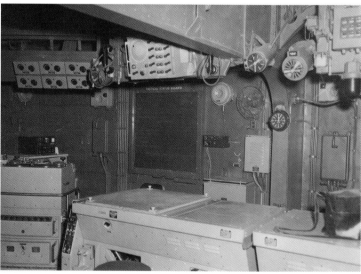

Part of the *Tennessee's* combat information center is seen facing forward in a January 21, 1945, photograph. On the bulkhead at the center is the tactical status board. Other equipment in the CIC included surface-search and air radar scopes, plotting boards, and radio and intercom sets. *National Archives*

This is the first in a series of photos of USS *Tennessee* upon departure from Puget Sound Navy Yard on January 25, 1945, following repairs and modernization. Most of the externally visible work accomplished that month comprised new paint overall and changes to some of the radar antennas. *National Archives*

The plain aspect of the *Tennessee*'s newly applied Measure 21 camouflage appears to advantage in this starboard broadside view. This scheme incorporated Navy Blue (5-N) on vertical surfaces and Deck Blue (20-B) on decks and other horizontal surfaces. *National Archives*

At the time the *Tennessee* was photographed off the bow on January 25, 1945, a long, gently curving, D-sectioned channel or fitting had been installed on the starboard side, near the bow. This feature, the purpose of which is not clear, may have dated to the repairs made after the collision with the *California*, and the feature remained a permanent part of the ship. *National Archives*

USS *Tennessee* is observed from astern in Puget Sound on January 25, 1945. In addition to being photographed from all angles on that date, the ship also retired to an anchorage off Blake Island in the sound, where its radar systems were recalibrated. *National Archives*

A tugboat nudges the *Tennessee* into position in Puget Sound on January 25, 1945. A feature not present on the ship when photographed at PSNY in January 1944 is a tall, rectangular plate spaced out a few inches from the side of the hull at around the break between the main deck and the upper deck; purpose unknown. *A. D. Baker III collection*

On January 27, 1945, the *Tennessee* conducts post-repair full-power trials in the Strait of Juan de Fuca. The ship passed all tests and was declared seaworthy. Two Kingfisher scout planes are aboard: one on the catapult and one alongside it on the fantail. *A. D. Baker III collection*

On the same date, the ship is observed broadside. A shadow cast by the aforementioned rectangular, vertically arranged plate is visible on the hull, below the rear edge of the aft twin 5-inch/38-caliber gun mount. The number "43" was painted on the bow and on the stern. *National Archives*

Tennessee is seen off its port bow on January 27, 1945. In addition to performing full-power trials on that date, the ship also passed through the Point Jefferson Degaussing Range, where the efficacy of the ship's equipment for reducing its magnetic signature (and thus reducing its vulnerability to magnetic mines) was measured. *National Archives*

The *Tennessee* cuts a beautiful wake on placid waters on January 27, 1945. Also during this date, the ship's 5-inch/38-caliber, 20 mm, and 40 mm antiaircraft gun batteries practiced firing at towed target sleeves. *National Archives*

In a final photo from the series taken January 27, 1945, the *Tennessee* is seen from astern. The ship's next stop would be the Hawaiian Islands on February 2. During this advance, the ship made an average speed of 17.5 knots. *National Archives*

A tugboat pushes the stern of USS *Tennessee* in Puget Sound after its January 1945 overhaul. In the distance are what appear to be two ferry boats. *USS Tennessee Museum*

This photo of a tugboat maneuvering against *Tennessee*'s stern apparently was taken within moments of the preceding one. Visible in both photos, but more so in the preceding one, are two taut chains running from the forecastle aft of the anchor to the forefoot under the bow, present in the preceding photo as well as in the series of photos taken January 25 and 27, 1945. These chains were for the purpose of rigging tow cables for paravanes, for cutting the tethering cables of submarine mines. *USS Tennessee Museum*

Less than a month after leaving Puget Sound Navy Yard, USS *Tennessee* has arrived in the vicinity of Iwo Jima on February 16, 1945, three days before the invasion is to begin. The ocean crossing had taken a terrible toll on the ship's new Measure 21 paint scheme, with discoloration and corrosion apparent all over the hull and some higher structures. *USS Tennessee Museum*

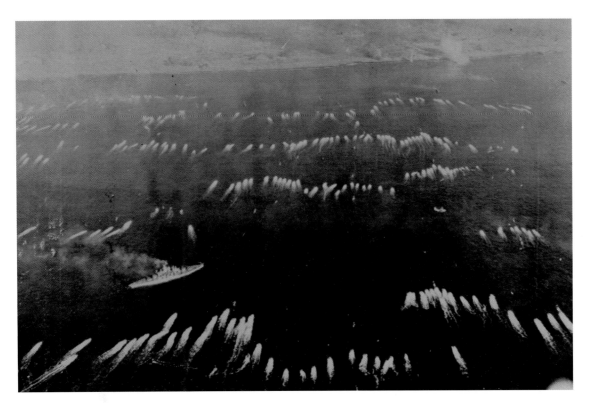

On D-day on Iwo Jima, February 19, 1945, waves of USMC amtracs head in toward the beaches as USS *Tennessee*, to the left of center, provides fire support. The bow of the battleship is oriented to the left. During the bombardment of the heavily defended island, an officer from the USMC 5th Amphibious Corps flew as an artillery spotter and observer in one of the *Tennessee*'s scout planes. *USS Tennessee Museum*

A Marine infantryman poses next to a Japanese bunker knocked out by shelling from the USS *Tennessee* on Iwo Jima. Although the bunker was constructed of heavily reinforced concrete, the battleship's shells pulverized it. *USS Tennessee Museum*

In an aerial photo possibly taken during the Operation Iceberg landings on Okinawa on April 1, 1945, smoke rises from USS *Tennessee* as landing craft pass it to the left. The ship had taken up station off Okinawa on March 26. On D-day, *Tennessee*'s number 7 quad 40 mm gun mount was shot up by Japanese aircraft, igniting ammunition and injuring six sailors. *USS Tennessee Museum*

While operating off the west coast of Okinawa during the midafternoon of April 12, 1945, Task Force 54, to which USS *Tennessee* was assigned, came under attack by a small group of kamikaze aircraft. Several of them targeted *Tennessee*, and one managed to crash onto the starboard side of the superstructure deck. A bomb carried by the plane broke free on impact and exploded. Casualties were twenty-nine dead and 129 wounded. Here, crewmen hose down number 7 quad 40 mm mount and nearby positions.
USS Tennessee Museum

Crewmen continue to hose down quad 40 mm mount number 9 in the aftermath of the April 12 kamikaze attack. Next to the splinter shield for the quad 40 mm guns is a smaller tub containing the Mk. 51 director for the 40 mm guns.
USS Tennessee Museum

The same sailor who is spraying water into quad 40 mm gun mount number 9 in the preceding photo is seen from another angle, on the quarter deck facing forward, as he continues to hose down the gun mount and splinter shield. *USS Tennessee Museum*

A crewman checks out the number 9 quad 40 mm gun mount and tub after they have been sufficiently sprayed. To the right rear of the gun mount is a spare 40 mm gun barrel and spring, grotesquely twisted and torn from the heat of the fire. Toward the right is the Mk. 51 director. In the foreground is the boom of the starboard boat crane. *USS Tennessee Museum*

Quad 40 mm gun mount number 7, on the starboard of the ship, received the brunt of the kamikaze attack. This view looks down and aft into the wreckage of the mount. Crewmen who survived the blast in this mount risked their lives by trying to save their wounded comrades and throwing ammunition overboard before it could explode. *USS Tennessee Museum*

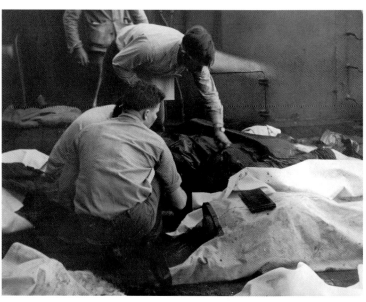

Crewmen of the *Tennessee* tend to the bodies of the men killed in action in the kamikaze attack on April 12, 1945. The remains would be buried at sea. *USS Tennessee Museum*

Personnel survey the destruction amidships on the starboard side of the *Tennessee* after the kamikaze attack on April 12, 1945. In the left foreground, the splinter shield of a 20 mm antiaircraft gun gallery was split open; above the top of the shield is a 20 mm gun barrel, twisted at a more than 90 degree angle. *USS Tennessee Museum*

On the day after the attack, forty-nine wounded crewmen were transferred from the *Tennessee* to the evacuation transport USS *Pinkney* (APH-2) for further treatment. Here, officers talk to wounded crewmen awaiting evacuation. *USS Tennessee Museum*

This undated photo of the *Tennessee* shows battle damage from the April 12, 1945, kamikaze attack but was taken before its May 1945 repairs at Ulithi. Inboard of the two rearmost twin 5-inch/38-caliber gun mounts on the starboard side are two 20 mm gun galleries, with the number 7 quad 40 mm gun mount between them, and substantial parts of the splinter shields of all three positions are missing. Also, pedestals for 20 mm guns are present in the aft position, but the guns are not mounted.
USS Tennessee Museum

One of the duties of battleships was to refuel smaller ships at sea. Here, a boom has been rigged on the deck of the *Tennessee* to support a fuel line to be passed over to the ship to the left. The scene was off the coast of Okinawa. *USS Tennessee Museum*

Sailors at sea wanted access to at least a few non-issue items during World War II; this especially included tobacco products, which were made available for purchase in the ship's store. *USS Tennessee Museum*

After the April 12 kamikaze attack, the *Tennessee* remained in Okinawan waters, although its starboard antiaircraft battery was greatly weakened. On May 3, it proceeded to Ulithi for repairs. There, on May 8, the battleship was moored to the repair ship USS *Ajax* (AR-6), as seen here; repairs on *Tennessee* lasted until May 23. *USS Tennessee Museum*

During the repairs at Ulithi, two new quad 40 mm antiaircraft gun mounts were installed to replace those destroyed in the April 12 attack. Several 20 mm gun mounts were installed, and there was a general repair and straightening of the starboard side of the ship where necessary. *Tennessee* departed from Ulithi on June 3, 1945. *USS Tennessee Museum*

USS *Tennessee* was based off Okinawa when the Japanese surrendered on September 2, 1945. Two weeks later, on September 16, a typhoon was reported to be approaching the area, and the *Tennessee* sortied out to the southwest to avoid the storm. This photo documents some of the rough seas the battleship encountered. *USS Tennessee Museum*

On September 22, 1945, the *Tennessee*, as Adm. Jesse B. Oldendorf's flagship, sailed with Task Unit 51.4.3 to Wakanoura Wan, Japan, to assist US occupation forces landing at Wakayama. *USS Tennessee Museum*

Tennessee crashes through huge waves during its efforts to avoid the brunt of a typhoon in mid-September 1945. The ship returned to Buckner Bay, Okinawa, where it dropped anchor at 0911 on September 18. *USS Tennessee Museum*

Here, Japanese VAdm. Hoka and his staff have arrived on the quarterdeck of the *Tennessee* to receive Adm. Oldendorf's terms of occupation. *USS Tennessee Museum*

On September 25, 1945, USS *Tennessee* is anchored in Wakanoura Wan, Japan. Now that active combat operations were over and the ship was operating in a harbor, more boats were carried on deck. For example, adjacent to the barbette of turret 3 is stowed a motorized boat with a light-colored cabin with three windows on the side. *National Archives*

CHAPTER 4
The End of the Line

On October 15, 1945, the *Tennessee* and its sister ship *California* departed from Japanese waters with Task Group 50.5 on their return voyage to the United States. The trip would not be a convenient passage to the West Coast, but rather a much-longer one to the East Coast via the Cape of Good Hope. One of the stops was at Colombo, Ceylon (now Sri Lanka), in October, where this photo of the ship with three USN destroyers moored alongside was taken. *National Archives*

Although some opined that the *Tennessee* should be the site of the Japanese surrender, since it was not only a Pearl Harbor survivor but had also fought in so many of the Pacific battles, that honor of course went to the *Iowa*-class battleship *Missouri*, named for President Truman's home state. Rather, when the Japanese surrendered on September 2, 1945, *Tennessee* was operating out of Buckner Bay, Okinawa, screening escort carriers and preparing for the possible invasion of the Japanese homeland.

Although the war was over, *Tennessee* and its men were not safe. On September 15, still off Okinawa, *Tennessee* was caught in a typhoon. Walls of water 60 feet high, pushed by winds clocked in excess of 65 knots, battered the ship. Men were tossed from their bunks as the ship rolled, coming dangerously close to capsizing. Fortunately, *Tennessee* was at sea, sparing it the fate that befell the armored cruiser *Memphis*.

Tennessee left Buckner Bay on September 18, bound for Wakayama/Wakanoura to accept the surrender of a local Japanese military installation. It arrived, along with sister ship *California*, on September 22. The Japanese delegation, led by VAdm. Hoka and RAdm. Yokai, was brought aboard and escorted to VAdm. Jesse Oldendorf's cabin, where the terms of occupation were laid out. On the twenty-fifth, thirty of *Tennessee*'s Marines and sailors joined US Army troops in going ashore as a reconnaissance party at Wakayama.

On September 3, *Tennessee*, accompanied by *California*, steamed into Tokyo Bay, mooring at the Yokosuka Naval Base. *Tennessee*'s sailors were granted liberty, and the Americans wandered Tokyo as well as the Japanese shipyard, including the relic battleship *Nagato*, now manned by an American prize crew.

Tennessee's men were eager to return home, and that welcome news came on October 14. VAdm. Oldendorf transferred his flag from *Tennessee* to the cruiser *Springfield* and radioed his former flagship this message:

> For the officers and men, we have been shipmates and been traveling a long, rough round together. Our efforts have been crowned with success. Now we have reached the parting of the way. May your return voyage and homecoming give you all the happiness you so richly deserve. Au revoir, Oldendorf.

Amazingly, despite having operated solely in the Pacific throughout the war, *Tennessee*, along with *California*, was ordered to Philadelphia.

The improvements made to both ships by Puget Sound following Pearl Harbor rendered both battleships too broad to transit the Panama Canal, meaning that to reach Philadelphia the ships would have to sail either around the tip of South America, or via the Indian Ocean and Africa.

Members of the *Tennessee*'s crew attend a religious service on the starboard side of the quarterdeck during the battleship's passage from Ceylon to Cape Town, South Africa. Visible from this angle are several of the antiaircraft gun mounts and splinter shields that were damaged in the April 12, 1945, kamikaze attack off Okinawa and were later repaired. *USS Tennessee Museum*

The ice cream stand, or gedunk, has been a popular diverson aboard large US warships since at least 1906, and the one aboard *Tennessee* was no exception. *USS Tennessee Museum*

On November 15, 1945, the task group of which USS *Tennessee* was part arrived at Cape Town, South Africa, for a brief layover during which the crew was allowed shore leave. The bright, white bloomers and muzzle covers on the 14-inch guns are noticeable. *USS Tennessee Museum*

During the return voyage to the United States in November 1945, the crew of turret 3 posed on the 14-inch guns for what they knew was going to be their last group portrait. In the background are two Kingfisher scout planes, fitted with covers over the canopies and cowlings. *USS Tennessee Museum*

Tennessee's final destination in its return voyage from Japan was Philadelphia Navy Yard, where the ship is seen arriving on a chilly December 7, 1945: auspiciously, four years to the day after Tennessee endured the Japanese attack on Pearl Harbor.
USS Tennessee Museum

The decision was made to sail through the Indian Ocean, and on October 15, 1945, *California* and the rest of Task Group 50.5 began the 16,000-mile trip to Philadelphia.

The long voyage was interrupted by sightseeing ports of call, including Singapore, Cape Town, and Colombo, Ceylon. It was there that *Tennessee*'s crew suffered one more casualty, when a sailor drowned while swimming in the Colombo harbor.

Finally, *Tennessee* reached the entrance to Delaware Bay off Cape May at noon on December 6, 1945. The next day, four years after it was attacked at Pearl Harbor, *Tennessee*, at 1250 hours, tied up at Philadelphia Naval Shipyard.

On May 8, 1946, *Tennessee* was pushed at a slight angle into Drydock 1 at the shipyard. Its sister ship was already in the drydock, at an opposite angle. The drydock was pumped out, and the sister ships came to rest on keel blocks, where they would remain for years. *Tennessee* was placed out of commission in reserve on February 14, 1947.

Its weapons and machinery were carefully preserved, and its spaces were sealed. Dehumidification equipment drew moisture from the air, retarding deterioration of the interior spaces. *Tennessee* awaited a call to return to arms that never came. The Korean War brought about the return to action of only the new *Iowa*-class battleships, but *Tennessee* and a host of other battleships remained in the reserve fleet.

On March 1, 1959, *Tennessee*, whose preservation status had been allowed to deteriorate as it became increasingly clear it would never return to service, was officially deemed obsolete and struck from the Naval Register.

On July 10, 1959, *Tennessee* was sold for scrap to the Bethlehem Steel Company for $724,999 and on July 26 left Philadelphia under tow, bound for the breaker's yard in Baltimore to be reduced to scrap.

USS *Tennessee*, left, and sister ship USS *California*, right, share Dry Dock No. 5 at Philadelphia Navy Yard, where they were being prepared for long-term storage, or "mothballing," in the spring of 1945–46. The gun ports of the 14-inch turrets have been fitted with molded seals. The 20 mm antiaircraft guns and mounts have been removed, the quad 40 mm gun mounts have been covered, and any hatches or fittings that could admit water were sealed. *National Archives*

USS *Tennessee* General Data, 1921

Builder	Brooklyn Naval Shipyard
Laid down	May 14, 1917
Launched	April 30, 1919
Commissioned	June 3, 1920

Dimensions

Length overall	624'
Waterline length	600'
Maximum beam	97' 5¾"
Max draft	31'
Displacement	32,300 long tons standard

Armor Protection

Total armor weight	14,541.8 tons
Belt	6" to 13.5"
Bulkheads	13.5"
Decks	70 lbs. special-treatment steel (STS) + 70 lbs. nickel steel; aft over steering; 180 lbs. STS + 70 lbs.
Turrets	Faceplates: 18" Roof: 5" Side: 10" Rear: 9"
Barbettes	13"
Conning tower	16" sides; 6" on top

Machinery

Boilers	Eight Babcock & Wilcox
Turbines	Two Westinghouse
Shaft horsepower	28,500 maximum ahead
Maximum speed	21.0 knots
Fuel capacity, design	4,656 tons oil, emergency
Endurance	10 knots: 20,500 nautical miles
Propellers	4
Rudders	One, balanced

Complement

Crew	1,146 total (50 officers; 1,026 enlisted, 70 Marines)

Armament

Main battery	12 14"/50-caliber Mark IV-I
Secondary battery	14 5"/50-caliber Mark VIII
Antiaircraft battery	Four 3"/50-caliber Mark X-2
Torpedo tubes	Two 21", Mark III-3
Landing gun	One 3"/23-caliber Mark XI
Machine guns	25 Browning .30-caliber, Model 1918; 12 Lewis .30-caliber, Model 1917
Rifles	350 Springfield, .30-caliber Model 1930
Pistols	123 Colt, .45-caliber, Model 1911

USS *Tennessee* General Data, April 1943

Dimensions

Length overall	624' 5"
Maximum beam	114' 0"
Max draft	33' 1"
Full load displacement	40,950 long tons

Armor Protection

Cruiser conning tower with 5" thick armor installed, second deck armor increased from 5" to 7". The 5" thick turret roof armor was replaced with new plates 7" thick as well.

Machinery

Boilers	Eight Babcock & Wilcox
Turbines	Two General Electric
Shaft horsepower	32,500 maximum ahead
Maximum speed	20.6 knots
Fuel capacity, full load	4,700 tons oil
Propellers	Four
Rudders	One, balanced

Complement

Crew	114 officers; 2,129 enlisted

Armament

Main battery	12 14"/50-caliber Mark IV-I
Secondary battery	16 5"/38-caliber
Antiaircraft battery	10 quad 40 mm; 43 20 mm

After being decommissioned in February 1947 and then spending the next twelve years in storage at Philadelphia, the *Tennessee* was sold for scrap to Bethlehem Steel in July 1959. Here, the ship is being towed from Philadelphia Navy Yard on its final trip, to Bethlehem's Baltimore facility, on July 23, 1959. *University of Memphis*

The *Tennessee* is under tow to Baltimore in July 1959. The ship exhibited years of neglect and lack of fresh paint. Most of the radar antennas had been removed long ago, but the antennas on the primary- and secondary-battery directors remained in place. *University of Memphis*

After arriving at Baltimore, the *Tennessee* rested at dock while it and its similarly fated sister ship *California* awaited breaking up. A heartfelt notation on this September 1959 photo of the *Tennessee* by P. H. Fields of the Third Division (or turret 3 crew) reads, "My last look and good by [*sic*] to a grand old Lady." *USS Tennessee Museum*

P. H. Fields captured another view of *Tennessee* from a closer perspective off the starboard bow at Baltimore in September 1959. The big number "43" had been painted on the bow sometime during the postwar years. *USS Tennessee Museum*

One last photo by P. H. Fields from September 1959 shows the aft turrets, including his old station, turret 3, where he served from 1938 to 1946. The *Tennessee* underwent the scrappers' torches starting in mid-April 1960. Thus ended an illustrious career that spanned from the dreadnought era to the nuclear age. *USS Tennessee Museum*

The original bell of USS *Tennessee*, dated 1920, is in the collections of the USS *Tennessee* Museum in Huntsville, Tennessee. This museum contains a sizeable collection of artifacts, photographs, and memorabilia connected to the battleship. *Author*